PETER HÜNERMANN

# HUMAN BEINGS ACCORDING TO CHRIST TODAY

Pope Francis' Anthropology

LIBERIA EDITRICE VATICANA

Published in Australia by

© Copyright 2019 Coventry Press

Coventry Press
33 Scoresby Road
Bayswater Vic. 3153
Australia

Original title: *Zur Frage nach der theologischen Antropologie in den lehramtlichen Verkundigungstexten von papst Franziskus*

Translated from German by Fabrizio Iodice
Translated into English by Salesians of Don Bosco of the Province of Mary Help of Christians of Australia and the Pacific

ISBN 9780987643179

© Copyright 2017 - Libreria Editrice Vaticana
00120 Città del Vaticano
Tel. 06.698.81032 - Fax 06.698.84716
commerciale.lev@spc.va

All rights reserved. Other than for the purposes and subject to the conditions prescribed under the *Copyright Act*, no part of this publication may be reproduced, stored in a retrieval system, or transmitted in any form or by any means, electronic, mechanical, photocopying, recording or otherwise, without the prior permission of the publisher.

Cataloguing-in-Publication entry is available from the National Library of Australia http:/catalogue.nla.gov.au/.

Printed in Australia

www.coventrypress.com.au

## SERIES
### *THE THEOLOGY OF POPE FRANCIS*

JURGEN WERBICK: *God's Weakness for Humankind.* Pope Francis' view of God

LUCIO CASULA: *Faces, Gestures and Places.* Pope Francis' Christology

PETER HÜNERMANN: *Human Beings According to Christ Today.* Pope Francis' Anthropology

ROBERTO REPOLE: *The Dream of a Gospel-inspired Church.* Pope Francis' Ecclesiology

CARLOS GALLI: *Christ, Mary, the Church and the Peoples.* Pope Francis' Mariology

SANTIAGO MADRIGAL TERRAZAS: *'Unity Prevails over Conflict'.* Pope Francis' Ecumenism

ARISTIDE FUMAGALLI: *Journeying in Love.* Pope Francis' Moral Theology

JUAN CARLOS SCANNONE: *The Gospel of Mercy in the Spirit of Discernment.* Pope Francis' Social Ethics

MARINELLA PERRONI: *Kerygma and Prophecy.* Pope Francis' Biblical Hermeneutics

PIERO CODA: *'The Church is the Gospel'.* At the sources of Pope Francis' theology

MARKO IVAN RUPNIK: *According to the Spirit.* Spiritual theology on the move with Pope Francis' Church

## ABBREVIATIONS

| | |
|---|---|
| AL | *Amoris Laetitia* |
| DV | *Dives in Misericordia* |
| EG | *Evangelii Gaudium* |
| EN | *Evangelii Nuntiandi* |
| GD | *Gaudium in Domino* |
| GS | *Gaudium et Spes* |
| LG | *Lumen Gentium* |
| LS | *Laudato Si'* |
| MV | *Misericordiae Vultus* |
| OT | *Optatam Totius* |
| PP | *Populorum Progressio* |
| SE | *Spiritual Exercises* |

# PREFACE TO THE SERIES

From the time of his first appearance in St Peter's Square on the evening of his election, it was more than clear that Francis' pontificate would be adopting a new style. His modest apparel, calling himself the Bishop of Rome, asking the people to pray for him – in the 'deafening silence' of a packed square – and greeting them with a simple '*buonasera*' (good evening) … these were all eloquent signs of the fact that there was a change taking place in the way the Pope related to people, and thus in the 'language' used.

The gestures and words that have followed from that occasion only confirm and strengthen this first impression. Indeed, it could be said that over the ensuing years, the image of the papacy has been decidedly transformed, involving a change that affects homilies, addresses and documents promulgated as well.

As could be predicted, this has generated divergent opinions, especially regarding his teaching. While many have in fact welcomed his magisterium with enthusiasm and deep interest, sensing the fresh wind of the gospel, some others have approached it in a more detached way and, at times, with suspicion. There has been no lack of more absolute views, even going as far as to doubt the existence of a theology in Francis' teaching.

A summary judgement of this kind could come from the very different backgrounds of Francis and his predecessor, Benedict XVI. The latter, we know, has been one of the most outstanding and important theologians of the twentieth century and undoubtedly relied on his personal theological development in his rich papal magisterium. We have not yet fully appreciated, nor will we cease to appreciate, the depth of this magisterium. What Bergoglio has behind him, on the other hand, is his long and deep-rooted experience as a religious and a pastor.

However, this does not mean that his magisterium is without a theology. The fact that he was not mostly, or only, a 'professional' theologian does not mean that his magisterium is not supported by a theology. Were this the case, we could say that, strictly speaking, the majority of his predecessors were without a theology, given that Ratzinger represents the exception rather than the rule.

In any case, the fact that we can discuss the theological significance of Francis' magisterium, as well as the fact that, very often, some of his highly evocative and very immediate expressions have been so abused as to rob them of their profundity – in the journalistic as well as the ecclesial ambit – makes the response of this series, which I have the honour of presenting, a significant one.

By drawing on the competence and rigorous study of theologians of proven worth, coming from diverse contexts, the series has sought to research the theological thinking which supports the Pope's teaching. It explores its roots, its freshness, and its continuity with earlier magisterium.

The result can be found in the eleven volumes which make up this series with its simple and direct title: 'The Theology of Pope Francis'.

They can be read independently of one another, obviously; they have been written by individual authors independently of each other. Nevertheless, the hope is that a reading of the entire series would not only be a valuable aid for grasping the theology upon which Francis' teaching is based, in the various theological fields of knowledge, but also an introduction to the key points of his thinking and teaching overall.

The intention, then, is not one of 'apologetics', and even less so is it to add further voices to the many already speaking about the Pope. The aim is to try to see, and to help others to see, what theological thinking Francis bases himself on and expresses, in such a fresh way in his teaching.

Among the many discoveries the reader could make in reading these volumes, would certainly be that of observing how so much of the beneficial freshness of the Council's teaching flows into Francis' magisterium. This is true both of the theological preparation he has had, and of what has followed from it. Given that it is perhaps still too soon for all this wealth to become common patrimony, peacefully and fully received by everyone, it should be no surprise that the Pope's teaching is sometimes not immediately understood by everyone.

By the same token, a point of no return has been reached in Francis' teaching, one that recent theology and the Council have both taught: that doctrine cannot be something extraneous to so-called pastoral theology and ministry. The truth that the Church is called to watch over is the truth of Christ's gospel, which needs to be communicated to the women and men of every time and place. This is why the task of the ecclesial magisterium must also be one of favouring this communication of the gospel. Hence, theology can never be reduced to a dry, desk-bound exercise, disconnected from the life of the people of God and its mission. This mission is that the women and men of every age encounter the perennial and inexhaustible freshness of Jesus' gospel.

Over these years there have been those who have heard some of Francis' own critical statements regarding theology or theologians, and have concluded that he holds it and them in low esteem. Perhaps a more detailed study of the Pope's teaching, such as offered by this series, could also be helpful for showing that, while we always need to be critical of a theology that loses its vital connection to the living faith of the Church, it is also essential to have a theology which takes up the task of thinking critically about this very faith, and doing so with 'creative fidelity', so that it may continue to be proclaimed.

Francis' teaching is certainly not lacking in a theology of this kind; and a theology of the kind is certainly one much desired by a magisterium such as his, which so wants God's mercy to continue to touch the minds and hearts of the women and men of our time.

Editor-in-chief<br>
Roberto Repole

# CONTENTS

Abbreviations ............................................................. 4
Preface to the Series .................................................... 5

### CHAPTER 1
### SOME PRIOR CONSIDERATIONS REGARDING METHOD .............................................................. 13
1. Introduction ................................................ 13
2. Considerations on the approach of this essay ... 23

### CHAPTER 2
### THE FUNDAMENTAL CHARACTERISTICS OF THEOLOGICAL ANTHROPOLOGY IN POPE FRANCIS' MAGISTERIAL DOCUMENTS .................... 27
1. *Being-in-the-world*: point of departure for the question of the human being in philosophical anthropology ..................... 27
2. How does this fundamental phenomenon show up in Pope Francis' theological anthropology? ....................................... 29
3. *Being-in-the-world*, based on and enlightened by the gospel: the point of approach for a modern theological anthropology .......................................... 34

## Chapter 3

### The second fundamental characteristic of modern anthropology: corporeality ..... 41

1. *The philosophical characterization of corporeality* ............................................ 41
2. *Observations on 'corporeality' in the context of papal magisterial documents* ... 46
3. *Observations on the phenomenon of corporeality in the post-synodal document,* Amoris Laetitia ................... 53

## Chapter 4

### The basic traits of 'corporeality' in the human being: affectivity, language, spirit and person in human being-there [*Da-sein*] ............................................................. 59

1. *Affectivity as a basic way of being human* .... 59
2. *On the linguistics of human existence* .......... 62
3. *Man: spirit and personhood* ......................... 71

## Chapter 5

### A look at the current situation given the basics of human existence ..................... 85

1. *Some prior notes on method* .......................... 85
2. *The current social scene from the point of view of theological anthropology* ............. 88

3. *The current social situation evaluated in* Evangelii Gaudium, Laudato Si' *and* Amoris Laetita.............................. 91

CONCLUDING NOTE................................................... 97

Chapter 1
# SOME PRIOR CONSIDERATIONS REGARDING METHOD

*1. Introduction*

If we consider the Encyclicals and Apostolic Exhortations published by Pope Francis since his election in 2013, we note the difference by comparison with corresponding statements by his predecessors. At the beginning of all his magisterial documents, Francis makes it clear that he is addressing everyone who believes in Christ: bishops, priests, deacons, members of consecrated life, the faithful, or – as in the case of *Laudato Si'* (*LS*), the Encyclical on the environment – world public opinion. He is not addressing theologians as such, or dealing with specific theological issues. Corresponding to this group of addressees, his magisterial texts feature a broadly figurative, narrative style. The Pope expressly recommends thoughtful reading and offers pointers for interpretation for individual groups who could be particularly interested in one or other chapter.[1]

---

1 Cf. POPE FRANCIS, Apostolic Exhortation *Evangelii Gaudium* (*EG*): "The joy of the Gospel fills the hearts and lives of all who encounter Jesus ... In this Exhortation I wish to encourage the Christian faithful to embark upon a new chapter of evangelization marked by this joy, while pointing out new paths for the Church's journey in years to come (*EG*, no. 1). "I have dealt extensively with these topics, with a detail which some might find excessive. But I have done so, not with the intention of providing an exhaustive

With regard to theological issues, Francis explains that given careful reading, the texts should be both plausible and acceptable.[2]

Given this approach, we only find a few sporadic notes, often consisting of basic statements by his predecessors, which emphasize or summarize the direction his reflections take. Besides, Pope Francis quite often differentiates his pastoral teaching from theological presentations, as occurred, for example, during his visit to the Lutheran church in Rome.

When the essay to follow speaks of theology in these texts of catechesis or proclamation, the question is not: 'Where did Pope Francis "get" this or the other wording from?' Theology develops the *ratio fidei* in a scientific way; *fides*, as found in the testimony or doctrine of faith of the Bishop of Rome, for which the principle holds true, as it does for other bishops, that 'The person who listens to you, listens to me.' There are also, clearly, other testimonies of faith in Scripture and Tradition. The designation of *ratio fidei* or *intellectus fidei* is something different from testimony, or the doctrines of the faith, or even catechetical teaching. The scientific work of theologians makes a contribution

---

treatise but simply as a way of showing their important practical implications for the Church's mission today. All of them help give shape to a definite style of evangelization which I ask you to adopt in every activity which you undertake" (*EG*, no. 18).

2  As suggested by Pope Francis in his note of response through his spokesperson, Fr Lombardi SJ, to the document presented by Cardinals R. Burke, C. Caffarra, W. Brandmüller, J. Meisner: "A request for clarification on some key points in *Amoris Laeetitia*", 19 September 2016.

to the clarification of the testimonies of faith for a proper understanding of the doctrine of faith through a critical, comparative examination of the many testimonies and doctrines of faith with their different authorities, their historical, cultural and philosophical conditioning through their respective hermeneutically relevant contexts. Depending on the different theological disciplines, different formal principles come into play. Critical reflections are part of these clarifications, warding off misunderstandings, introducing distinctions which allow believers to employ their own efforts and beliefs and thus better appreciate the roots of their faith. What significance does this have for the reflections that follow? Does it make sense to speak of a theological anthropology in Pope Francis' kerygmatic texts?

By contrast with Pope Benedict XVI, Pope Francis is not a teacher of dogmatic theology who has given classes in theology over many years and written corresponding theological treatises, such that he can start out from 'his theology' and from his debates with other theologians.

Naturally, Pope Francis has a theological formation. As a Jesuit he studied philosophy and theology. He says, as a result of his theological studies which he finished before Vatican Council II: 'Human beings are in search of themselves, and, of course they can also make mistakes in this search. The church has experienced times of brilliance, like that of Thomas Aquinas. But the church has also lived through times of decline in its ability to think. For example, we must not confuse the genius of Thomas Aquinas with the age of decadent Thomist commentaries. Unfortunately, I studied philosophy from textbooks that came from decadent or largely bankrupt Thomism. In thinking of the human being, therefore, the church should strive for genius and not for decadence.'[3]

In the quoted interview, the Pope is silent on his theological studies, which he pursued between 1965 and 1969. These were years of great theological research, but what path did this research take? Theological reflection in Latin America found itself faced with absolutely new questions, and the manuals the Jesuits used were of no use for these. But what was the nub of the new questions assailing students and teachers of theology over these years, especially in Latin America? The documents of Vatican II, especially *Gaudium et Spes* (*GS*), but also *Lumen Gentium* (*LG*), the Constitution on Divine Revelation, and other decrees like the one on the laity, missions etc., emphasised the fundamental mission of the Church in the world, and precisely in an effort that takes in all the dimensions of activity and human life in the world here and now. Now, the public contexts in Latin America, including in Argentina in this period, were in real turmoil. Just a few weeks prior to John XXIII announcing the Council in January 1959, Fidel

---

3 A Spadaro SJ, Interview with Pope Francis, available at https://w2.vatican.va/content/francesco/en/speeches/2013/september/documents/papa-francesco_20130921_intervista-spadaro.html. At the time, Jesuit philosophical studies were rigorously controlled. The structure was pre-established at international level: *philosophia scholastica; logica, critica; metaphysica generalis; psychologia, cosmologia, theodicea; there was also the history of philosophy and scientific questions inherent to philosophy.*

Castro entered Havana, and nuclear war between the USA and the Soviets was only just avoided in 1962. The social and political situation in Latin America worsened overall. In 1964 – immediately before Bergoglio's theological studies – there was a military coup in Brazil against President Goulart, who sought to undertake profound social reform in that country. Frey came to power in Chile with a reform program which also projected a fundamental transformation in the social conditions of the country. In April 1965, the USA invaded the Dominican Republic. In February 1966, Columbian priest Camillo Torres was murdered. He was a symbolic figure for the Columbian guerilla movement. Still in 1966, there was a military coup in Argentina. The breeding ground for these social and political battles was the poverty and social exclusion of large groups of the population, illiteracy and misery among rural populations and, at the same time, the inadequacy of so-called liberalism.

Inspired by the Second Vatican Council, the Latin American Church focused on a '*pastoral de conjunto*', a joint or integral pastoral ministry which addressed the burning issues in Latin American society to remedy them in the spirit of the gospel. This is the framework for the founding of a number of groups of priests. 'Priests for the Third World' came into existence in Argentina; 'Christians for Socialism' was set up in Chile, involving priests and laity; a group inspired essentially by the 'theory of dependence'[4] formed

---

4 Theories of dependence developed by A.C. Frank; C. Furtrado; Th. Dos Santos; F.H. Cardosso; F. Faletto and other sociologists.

around Gustavo Gutierrez. The names clearly describe the ways in which priests and religious, above all, perceived the situation for large sectors of the population and posed the question of the Church's mission. The view of Church taught in the dominant traditional theology was seen as an abstract and ideological scheme. The 'Exodus' became an inspiring symbol, and 'liberation' – often with 'integral' added to it – became the distinctive feature of the understanding of faith.

The Second Latin American Synod met in Medellín in 1968. In 2007, Gustavo Gutierrez described the significance of this ecclesial meeting thus: 'The result of the impetus of the Council and shaped by the historical situation that the continent was experiencing at the time, the Synod set itself the task of considering the human and social reality, reflecting on and offering criteria for proclaiming the Gospel in the light of the Council's message.'[5] Questions of the kind that were occupying the minds of students of theology found no response in the traditional dogmatic treatises, nor was there any place they could be posed in the theological setting. The need arose, then, for a new kind of theology, a theology of liberation with its own methodology, a new approach to christology, ecclesiology, the doctrine of the sacraments and ecclesial ministry.

While the Council's message in Europe was the result of a broad theological and pastoral work of reform aimed at a corresponding renewal of the Church, Vatican II's impetus

---

5   G GUTIERREZ, in S SCATENA, *In populo pauperum – la Chiesa latino-americano dal Concilio a Medellín (1962-1968)* Il Mulino, Bologna 2007, XI.

in Latin America took a different direction, essentially of a socio-ecclesiological and political kind. Later – after the end of the Pinochet era – the Chilean bishops would speak of a climate of 'political messianism'. Theological development as part of this impetus was a longer process, leading essentially to the discovery of popular religion as a theological application or place in its own right. It also saw basic communities which featured protest as a distinctive mark from the outset. They were strongly encouraged in Argentina by groups of younger theologians from the Catholic Faculty of Theology in Buenos Aires – not by the Jesuit Faculty of Theology – which had formed around Lucio Gera.[6] Over these years, the Jesuit Higher Institute of Philosophy and Theology and the Argentinian Jesuit Province had been torn by a number of bitter disputes and losses. This explains why, immediately after his priestly ordination, Fr Bergoglio was sent to Spain for his tertianship and appointed novice master immediately upon his return (at the beginning of 1972) and, shortly afterwards, as Rector of the Higher Institute of Philosophy and Theology as well as a council member for the Jesuit Province in Argentina. Immediately after his solemn profession he was elected Provincial on 31 June 1973. After serving the six year period in that office he was chosen once more as Rector of the Higher Institute (1980-1986). It was such a turbulent time for the Jesuits in Argentina

---

6  During his interview with Antonio Spadaro, other than Henri de Lubac and Michel de Certaux Pope Francis speaks explicitly of Lucio Gera as one of the most significant theologians for him.

that they had to have recourse to foreign superiors. These years left no room for further work in theological research and specialisation. An attempt to write a doctoral thesis on Romano Guardini in Frankfurt was quickly interrupted.

In retrospect, Pope Francis has emphasized the decisive assistance that Ignatian discernment of spirits offered him along this journey. It led him out of a poor managerial style – the result of inexperience – as well as some inner insecurity connected with the profoundly new direction taken by the Society of Jesus under its General, Fr Arrupe, and the theology of liberation which was beginning to take shape.

'Discernment of spirits' also seems to have been Jorge Bergoglio's most important aid in relationship to theological issues which he was inevitably faced with as Provincial and Rector of the Higher Institute. His understanding of this discernment came essentially from Ignatius himself. Bergoglio also nominates Peter Fabro in particular, Ignatius' Savoyan room mate during the time of his studies in Paris. Michel de Certaux, whom Bergoglio quotes similarly as being among the confreres of the Order who formed him, had commented on Fabro's 'Memorial', describing him as the 'reformed priest'.[7]

The mystical interpretation of life and the *Spiritual Exercises* (*SE*) by Jesuits Louis Lallemant (1578-1635) and Jean Joseph Serin (1600-1665) did not lead Bergoglio

---

7  P FABRO, *Memorial. Traduit et commenté par Michel de Certaux SJ*, Desclée De Brouwer, Paris 1960. Bergoglio seems to recognise himself in Fabro's vocational and professional choice. Cf. *Ibidem*, nos 10-14, cit., 112-115. Fabro's unreserved involvement in pastoral service has been a living model for him.

only to Fabro. They also gave him an inner bond with the theological approach of Henri de Lubac. Under the influence of Blondel's fertile mind, de Lubac proposed:

- A systematic theological notion of the historical orientation of the human being towards God (Surnaturel), which led him to a theological dialogue with various forms of atheism;
- an ecclesiology characterized by trinitarian theology which has permeated the history of humankind, combined with an analysis of the spiritual situation of modernity;
- a christology which picks up on the cosmic approaches of Teilhard de Chardin.

In de Lubac, all this is bound up with some profound understandings of the history of the theology from antiquity (*Sources chrétiennes*) and harsh criticism of Neo-scholastic and Neo-thomist positions and their narrow perspectives. When Bergoglio reconnects with de Lubac, he does not do so by recalling the many detailed studies of the history of theology by this learned Jesuit but rather the fundamental directions underlying his theology which lead him beyond the narrow approaches of Neo-scholasticism.

Pope Francis finally refers to Father Arrupe and a certain initial uncertainty regarding him. In my view, this note is not a reference to his interpretation of the Second Vatican Council or to his judgement on the epoch-making changes brought about by modernity and the critical situation of the

Church in this context.[8] The 'uncertainties' seem to me to refer to the changes in lifestyle of the communities, which for the young and as yet inexperienced Provincial and Rector of the Higher Institute, meant a huge challenge during those turbulent years in Argentina. If we look at Father Arrupe's central texts on the Council, on the needs of the Church, its mission in following Christ which had to be carried out today in society, and compare them with Bergoglio's texts, it becomes evident that the similarity between them often goes even as far as the choice of words.[9]

The way in which Pope Francis reacts to the demands of his position with regard to Vatican II shows that for many years the realization of the Council has been one of the great spiritual imperatives of his pastoral practice. 'To get to the point, the Holy Spirit annoys us, because he moves us, he makes us travel, he pushes the Church forward ... We would like the Holy Spirit to doze off ... We want to subdue the Holy Spirit ... Just one example: let's think of the Council. The Council was a wonderful work of the Holy Spirit... But 50 years later, have we done everything the Holy Spirit

---

8  When he took up his role, the Jesuit General, elected in 1965, took up the Council's requests with extraordinary vigour, demanding a corresponding critical presence of the Order guided by the inspiring words of justice, commitment to the poor and their dignity and formation, and human rights. At the same time he set in motion a change in the lifestyle of the Jesuits in terms of greater mutual integration between spirituality and apostolate.

9  On this, cf. P ARRUPE, *Unser Zeugnis muss glaubwürdig sein. Ein Jesuit zu den Problemen von Kirche und Welt am Ende des 20. Jahrhundert. Mit einem Vorwort von Karl Rahner*, Ostfildern 1981, and the arguments pursued by Pope Francis in *EG*.

told us in the Council? In that continuity of growth of the Church that was the Council? No. We celebrate this anniversary, we build a monument, but we don't want it to bother us.'[10]

Or, during an interview, he answered the question as to why the Council is not quoted more often: 'It is useless quoting it, which only helps its enemies. What's needed is to do it.'[11]

*2. Considerations on the approach of this essay*

Pope Francis is a pastor with a theological formation who essentially tackles even theological issues through discernment of spirits. So in what sense and with what approach can we then construct the theological anthropology that lies behind his proclamation or *kerygma*? In what follows, we will allow ourselves to be guided by the notion that in many details, Bergoglio's magisterial texts reflect a sharing in specialist theological discussion and developments in modern theology which he, as a pastor with theological formation and thus very much alert to theological discussion, has taken up and made his own. In what follows, therefore, we would like to begin from Gabriel Amengual's *Antropología filosófica*.[12] He is a priest and philosopher from Mallorca, particularly interested in the

---

10   Homily on 16 April 2013 at Santa Marta.
11   P RODARI, "I due Papi: La fede non si impone con la violenza", in *La Repubblica*, 6 July 2013.
12   G AMENGUAL, *Antropología filosófica*, Biblioteca de Autores Cristianos, Madrid 2007.

philosophical anthropology of the last hundred years and is at the same time an excellent fundamental theologian. This volume of the *Sapientia rerum* series of the *Biblioteca de Autores Cristianos* has been well received in the world of Latin American studies, especially in the theological formation area.

We will adopt Amengual's way of structuring things. Following an introduction on the history of philosophy of the kind that Scheler has called (1927) 'Philosophical anthropology',[13] the title of the first part, 'Being-in-the-

[13] An excellent overview of the historical development of philosophical anthropology from Plato and Aristotle to Malebranche and Leibniz is offered by Odo Marquardt in his article: *Anthropologie*, in HWPH, 1, 362-363, which takes up this period by adopting the definition of Abbé Mallet (1778): "Manière de s'exprimer, par laquelle les écrivains sacrés attribuent à Dieu des parties, des actions ou des affections qui ne conviennent qu'aux hommes et cela pour s'accomoder et se proportionner à la faiblesse de notre intelligences" (A way of expressing ourselves, in which the sacred writers attribute to God stances, actions or sentiments which are only of value to human beings, and this in order to stoop to the level of weakness of our understanding).

(A Mallet, *Anthropologie*, in *Encyclopédie ou Dictionnaire raisonné* 1778). For further development, Marquardt quotes the German philosophical school from the end of the seventeenth century until the end of the eighteenth, and Wolf, the English and French 'moralistic' approach of philosophical and moral anthropology, ending with empirical anthropological research into the 'natural' properties of the human being: sex, age, temperament, character, race. For Kant, 'anthropology', which he understands as 'an understanding of the world which we arrive at neither through purely metaphysical thinking nor naturalistic experiment but only through common experience' (*Ibidem*, 365a), marks the turning point toward a critical phase.

Beginning with German idealism – Schelling, Hegel, Feuerbach

world' deals with *the structure or essential features of human existence*, through 'Corporeality', 'Language', 'Socialization', 'Conscience and spirit', 'The person'. In the second part, Amengual describes what specifies the human being as such: the formation of personal identity, the realization and achievement of freedom, action, historical realization and development of culture and society. Then the third part is dedicated to the limitations of being human: evil, the fall, sin and death.

Here we will focus on the chapter: 'Essential features of human existence', since it deals with the foundations of modern anthropology. The arguments on what specifies our being human deal with the theological perspectives which immediately flow from these essential features. Indeed, these essential features are forms of realization of human existence. Corresponding to the third part of Amengual's work would be the theology of sin, soteriology and eschatology. But in such a brief summary it would not be possible to take up these notions.[14]

---

and Marx – a new stage begins: reflection on anthropology involving history, culture and lifestyles up to the turning point of modernity, begun by Cheller, Heidegger, French phenomenology, Plessner, Gehlen etc. This becomes Amengual's point of departure.

14 We would like to offer a further recap: under the title of '*sociabilidad*', the author presented an extensive review of traditional kinds of social philosophy and then very various modern discussions on identity, selfhood, otherness, forms of recognition, understanding of society, community, intersubjectivity, individualism, collectivism, etc. Except for a handful of abstract reflections, there is no exploration of some fundamental trait of human existence. Thus the author speaks of the principle of

At the beginning of each chapter we will offer a brief sketch of the corresponding arguments in *Antropología filosófica*. This is not meant to be an exact and exhaustive effort to present Amengual's concepts and emphases. Rather does his work serve as a comparison in general terms. In individual points the author allows himself to introduce some additions of his own, especially ones coming from very recent phenomenological research. In the second part, in each chapter we will be looking for traces and reflections of these fundamental characteristics in Pope Francis' catechetical and theological arguments in the magisterial documents quoted earlier.

---

subsidiarity and solidarity, competitive, corporate and systematic relationships (cf. G AMENGUAL, *Antropología filosófica, cit.*, 143-166). We have omitted some of the presentations.

CHAPTER 2
# THE FUNDAMENTAL CHARACTERISTICS OF THEOLOGICAL ANTHROPOLOGY IN POPE FRANCIS' MAGISTERIAL DOCUMENTS

*1. Being-in-the-world: point of departure for the question of the human being in philosophical anthropology*

In the case of Max Scheler, the question of philosophical anthropology was formulated in the 1920s when it had matured and become urgent. Earlier, for example Dilthey, it had focused on the question of man's being in terms of his historicity, and had sought to develop an 'inner psychology' of the human being as the foundation for the human sciences. Scheler put it this way: 'After some two thousand years of "history", our era is the first in which man has become totally himself and "problematic": he does not know who he is, but knows that he does not know this!'[1] Until the recent period of history, human beings were the centre of reality. This held both for our view of the cosmos and our position amongst beings and their ordering, such as plants and animals. From this came the metaphysical doctrine of the soul, as proposed by Aristotle for example. The loss of this central position due to changes in the world and historical experience in the modern era and in modernity, the development of science and improvements in agriculture, craftsmanship and modern

---

1  Cf. *Ibidem*, 5.

technology, the loss of the natural onto-theological ties to God, present us with an indefinable philosophical question regarding man's being, one which cannot be objectified or described. Hence the first essential feature of the human being is his being-there [*Da-sein*], his being present in the world. This presence in the world is the basic condition. Parallel with Scheler's reflections on the 'position of man in the cosmos', and those of Husserl on the 'vital world' and the 'crisis of European sciences', Martin Heidegger published Being and Time, in which he speaks of being-in-the-world as an existential circumstance of man, that is, a definition which is not specific, not objectifiable. Referring to Heidegger, Scheler speaks of man's 'constitutive openness' to the world, but both are referring to the same phenomenon: man's being-there is his being-in-the-world [*In der Welt-sein*]. Merleau-Ponty reveals that this original relationship is determined by the body through which language, perception and understanding of the world are formed.[2]

Amengual explains this fundamental phenomenon by recalling the ways Scheler, Husserl, Heidegger and Merleau-Ponty analyze this primordial condition from the point of view of its essential moments. In the process, all the differences between the four great phenomenologists are picked up, since it deals with structural moments which structure this fundamental phenomenon, moments which are then tackled in turn by the various chapters in the first part: the 'corporeality of human existence [*Da-sein*]',

---

2 Cf. B. WALDENFELS, *Phänomenologie in Frankreich*, Suhrkamp Verlag, Frankfurt 1983, 142-217.

'affectivity', 'language', 'being-with [*Mit-sein*]', 'conscience' and 'spirit' and finally the 'personal character' of man's *Dasein* or being-there.

## 2. How does this fundamental phenomenon show up in Pope Francis' theological anthropology?

The first question that arises regarding Pope Francis' theological anthropology is: how does *Evangelii Gaudium* (*EG*), Pope Francis' basic program for his pontificate, reflect this fundamental phenomenon? That is, this phenomenon which has been revealed and described by phenomenologists of modernity with the term 'being-in-the-world'?

To respond to the question we will not refer to quotations from Scheler, Husserl, Heidegger and Merleau-Ponty. This would only give us theory, but without developing and exploring this essential phenomenon. The question is: how do Pope Francis' arguments focus attention on this essential phenomenon – which all these phenomenologists maintain is hidden and can only be revealed with effort?

If we begin with the title of this magisterial document from Pope Francis, we get our first clue: he adds to the first two words of the introduction, 'The joy of the Gospel', the comment that this work deals with 'The proclamation of the Gospel in today's world'. 'Gospel' here does not mean one of the four Gospels, but the word of God, 'the gospel he promised beforehand through his prophets in the Holy Scriptures, the gospel concerning his Son' (Rom 1:2-3). This Gospel, which determines the existence of the human being in faith in today's world, is the subject of this program.

Today's world is expressly defined as an historical world which encourages Christians to 'a new chapter of evangelization.' It deals with a message of salvation and joy to point to the message of salvation and joy of God in today's world, and 'paths for the Church's journey in years to come' (*EG*, no. 1).

How does this beginning shape the structure of *EG*? In order to recognize this particular emphasis, it could be of assistance to compare it with the Pastoral Constitution *Gaudium et Spes* (*GS*), which begins with an introductory description of man's circumstances in today's world and explains the changed conditions of life for people today: social, psychological, moral and religious transformations. The Pastoral Constitution speaks of imbalances in today's world and points to the more general aspirations of humankind as well as human beings' deeper questions. This is the historical and sociological introduction. The first three chapters of *GS* then deal with 'The dignity of the human person', 'The community of mankind', 'Man's activity throughout the world'. The arguments it refers to are key and decisive issues for philosophical anthropology dealt with in Gabriel Amengual's text based on philosophical sources. While not quoting the Pastoral Constitution, Amengual touches on and at least in part introduces the topics presented in the three chapters of *GS* just mentioned.[3] At the end of each of the three chapters of *GS* comes a section with a christological approach. Thus, at the end of the part

---

[3] Cf. for example *GS*, no. 15 on intellect and wisdom, and no. 17 on freedom.

on human dignity, it says in *GS* no. 22: 'The truth is that only in the mystery of the incarnate Word does the mystery of man take on light. For Adam, the first man, was a figure of Him Who was to come, namely Christ the Lord. Christ, the final Adam, by the revelation of the mystery of the Father and His love, fully reveals man to man himself and makes his supreme calling clear. It is not surprising, then, that in Him all the aforementioned truths find their root and attain their crown.'[4] The testimony of Christian faith is thus added under the form of a statement specific to essential philosophical analysis by phenomenologists. In the final reflections of the first part of *GS*, in the fourth chapter, this juxtaposition is described as the process of mutual learning between the Church and the world. The result is described by listing the things that the world must learn from the Church and vice versa.

The very same basic structure is offered in the second part of *GS*, just that in this case, by contrast with the first part, it makes special mention of urgent problems such as the promotion of the dignity of marriage and family, the proper promotion of culture, questions regarding socio-economic life, the political community and promotion of peace in the progress made by the international community. What is not taken into consideration in *GS* is the primordial nature of the phenomenon of being-there, being-in-the-

---

4  P HÜNERMANN, *Die Dokumente des II. Vatikanischen Konzils,* Freiburg i. Br. 2004. 621ff [an English translation can be found at http://www.vatican.va/archive/hist_councils/ii_vatican_council/documents/vat-ii_const_19651207_gaudium-et-spes_en.html]

world, corporeal being [*Leibhaftig-sein*] which is the basis *par* excellence for any knowledge, experience, appearance of reality and how it is constituted. Only this way can there be faith: the Church *in the world*, communicated by its bodily being-there. There are not two separate entities involved here, two independent entities that can learn about each other. The Council Fathers did not know or recognize the 'transcendental level' of phenomenological analysis,[5] in which one is recognized in the other and through the other. Accusations later levelled at the Pastoral Constitution are clearly tied to this shortcoming. The Constitution does not say that for Christians the world is a place of temptation and threat, and its critics point out the lack of the profession of faith in the cross of Jesus Christ: 'by which the world has been crucified to me, and I to the world' according to Paul (cf. Gal 6:14).

Pope Francis has another approach to that of *GS*. In *EG*, the document laying out the program for his entire pontificate, he speaks directly of the gospel and its

---

5  In his introduction to *Being and Time*, Martin Heidegger explicitly notes: 'Being, as the basic theme of philosophy, is no class or genus of entities; yet it pertains to every entity. Its "universality" is to be sought higher up. Being and the structure of Being lie beyond every entity and every possible character which an entity may possess. Being is the transcendens pure and simple. And the transcendence of *Dasein's* Being is distinctive in that it implies the possibility and the necessity of the most radical individuation. Every disclosure of Being as the transcendens is transcendental knowledge. Phenomenological truth (the disclosedness of Being) is *veritas transcendentalis*.' (*Being and Time*, Tr. by John Macquarries and Edward Robinson, HarperCollinsPublishers 2008, or German: Sein und Zeit, Tübingen 1953, 38).

inseparable joy. The term 'gospel' describes God's provident word through which the world and man have been given and which is at the same time addressed substantially to man in his being-in-the-world. The gospel is the word in which and for which being-in-the-world exists, the *Da-sein*, the existence of human beings. With this assumption, from the outset of his arguments Francis is moving within the context of philosophical anthropology: he is reflecting on the primordial phenomenon – the human being exists, and the human being-in-the-world exists. But from the outset he is reflecting on this in the 'light of faith', in the light of the gospel.

At the beginning of his pontificate, Francis spoke of the gospel as the 'light of faith' in the Encyclical *Lumen Fidei* (*LF*), 29 June 2013:[6] 'The light of faith is unique, since it is capable of illuminating every aspect of human existence ... Faith is born of an encounter with the living God who calls us and reveals his love, a love which precedes us and upon which we can lean for security and for building our lives. Transformed by this love, we gain fresh vision, new eyes to see; we realize that it contains a great promise of fulfilment, and that a vision of the future opens up before us. Faith, received from God as a supernatural gift, becomes a light for our way, guiding our journey through time' (*LF*, no. 4). In the encounter with Jesus Christ we look back over that provident word in history, wherein the meaning and fullness of existence in the world shines out, the meaning to which human beings tend for the simple fact that they exist in the world.

6  Cf. http://w2.vatican.va/content/francesco/en/encyclicals/documents/papa-francesco_20130629_enciclica-lumen-fidei.html

> The joy of the gospel fills the hearts and lives of all who encounter Jesus. Those who accept his offer of salvation are set free from sin, sorrow, inner emptiness and loneliness. With Christ joy is constantly born anew ... a joy ever new, a joy which is shared (*EG*, no. 1)

Thus we have provided an answer to the question of what the approach and departure point is for the modern theological anthropology which shines through the kerygmatic texts of Pope Francis.

## 3. *Being-in-the-world, based on and enlightened by the gospel: the point of approach for a modern theological anthropology*

So that this response is not substantially misunderstood, and so that we do not simply see the phenomenological approach as a slightly altered metaphysical doctrine on God, or in other words an onto-theological doctrine, we will briefly take up here some pointers from Heidegger and Scheler in their research into the place of the sacred or the divine in the world. In his famous letter on humanism to Jean Beaufret, Heidegger speaks of the 'homelessness' [*Heimatlosigkeit*] of modern man as shown, among other things, by the phenomena of man's alienation from himself in Marx's thinking. Heidegger sees the necessity of investigating the truth of being: 'Only from the essence of the holy is the essence of divinity to be thought of. Only in the light of the essence of divinity can it be thought or said what the word 'God' is to signify. Or, should we not first be able to hear and understand all these words carefully if we are to be permitted as men, that is, as *eksistent* creatures, to experience a relation of God to man?'[7]

In his lecture 'The Thing', Heidegger speaks of heaven and earth, divinities and mortals. 'The divinities are the beckoning messengers of the godhead. Out of the hidden sway of the divinities the god emerges for what he is, which removes him from any comparison with beings that are present ... The mortals are human beings. They are called mortals because they can die. To die means to be capable of death as death. Only man dies. The animal perishes. It has death neither ahead of itself nor behind it. Death is the shrine of Nothing, that is, of that which in every respect is never something that merely exists, but which nevertheless *presences*, even as the mystery of Being itself. As the shrine of Nothing, death harbours within itself the *presencing* of Being ... Mortals are who they are, as mortals, present in the shelter of Being. They are the *presencing* relation to Being as Being.'[8]

Emanuel Lévinas, pupil and critic of Heidegger, expresses the original experience of the divine of which Heidegger speaks, by consciously shifting the emphasis from reflection on being to experience of the face of the other. It is here that the nameless call of the 'Other' occurs *par excellence*, which makes human beings responsible, a call we cannot ignore.

---

[7]  M Heidegger, *Letter on Humanism*. A number of English translations are available. This one is from http://globalvisionpub.com/globaljournalmanager/pdf/1393650768.pdf

[8]  M Heidegger, 'The Thing' in *Poetry, Language, Thought* 1971, tr. By Albert Hofstader, published 2013 by Harper Perennial Modern Classics.

It comes down to a structure analogous to Heidegger's: the human being, as an accountable being, is a being of liberty [*Freiheitswesen*] in what is intangible, incomprehensible *par excellence*, in the Other par excellence.[9] In his late work *On the Eternal in Man*, Max Scheler deals with the divine, but without referring to the distinction we find in Heidegger between actual being and Being:

> This unconditional self-inclusion in the sphere of relative being – to the last jot of selfhood – is the foremost characteristic in the religious conception of this first attribute of divinity. On this point there is no reservation on the ground of distinctions between soul and body, spirit and flesh, I and thou, etc. No; utter dependence affects the human being as an undivided whole, as a simple fragment of this 'world' – 'world' being the heading under which man subsumes the totality of relative being. In the religious conception of this primary content of the divine essence there is no question either of an 'inference' or of any theoretical, philosophical perception, such as underlies the 'proof from contingency' … But here too, as everywhere, 'to stand revealed' means to have been the reverse of extrapolated, inferred, abstracted. It means that when the absolute being of an object qualified as 'divine' becomes, of and out of itself, 'transparent' and 'trans-lucent' (in the active senses)

---

9   Similar to the two examples given here, Amengual presents the fundamental parallels in Merleau-Ponty or Paul Ricoeur

within an empirical object from the relative sphere, it is only the operation of shining and looking through which lifts the latter object into prominence and singles it out from among all other objects of relative existence.[10]

If we start out from these pieces of information from the phenomenologies of Heidegger up to Ricoeur and beyond, and then look at *EG*, it seems clear how Pope Francis corresponds to this basic viewpoint. This can be clearly shown in the first two numbers of the introduction, including the first section: 'A joy ever new, a joy which is shared' and the second 'The delightful and comforting joy of evangelizing'.

Francis speaks (*EG*, no. 2) of 'the voice of God' and 'the quiet joy of his love'. He encourages Christians 'everywhere, at this very moment' to a renewed personal encounter with Jesus Christ, or at least to decide to let him encounter them. He asks them to do this unfailingly each day. Listening to God's voice, however, and taking 'a step towards Jesus,' people come to realize that he is already there, 'waiting for us with open arms.' 'God never tires of forgiving us; we are the ones who tire of seeking his mercy.' 'No one can strip us of the dignity bestowed upon us by this boundless and unfailing love' (*EG*, no. 3).

The joy we experience from this love of God is of a particular kind: '... I realize of course that joy is not expressed the same way at all times in life, especially at

---

10   M SCHELER, *On the Eternal in Man*, Translated from the German *Vom Ewigen im Menschen,* SCM Press 1960, 164-165.

moments of great difficulty. Joy adapts and changes, but it always endures, even as a flicker of light born of our personal certainty that, when everything is said and done, we are infinitely loved. I understand the grief of people who have to endure great suffering, yet slowly but surely we all have to let the joy of faith slowly revive as a quiet yet firm trust, even amid the greatest distress' (*EG*, no. 6). The attitudes and ways of acting that are thus overcome, Francis calls 'a blunted conscience', an 'interior life ... caught up in its own interests and concerns', the lack of an 'authentic source of personal realization.' 'life is attained and matures in the measure that it is offered up in order to give life to others. This is certainly what mission means' (*EG*, nos. 2, 10).

All these are attitudes and ways of acting that are rooted in the temptation to give ourselves over to the many kinds of amusements in today's technological society, and to constantly make excuses so we can put conditions on God's voice and not follow it. God's voice, instead, leads to continuous change and an increasingly more profound creativity.

This is what Francis means by 'The New Evangelization for the Transmission of the Christian Faith', and it is up to Christians, who 'have the duty to proclaim the Gospel without excluding anyone. Instead of seeming to impose new obligations, they should appear as people who wish to share their joy, who point to a horizon of beauty and who invite others to a delicious banquet. It is not by proselytizing that the Church grows, but "by attraction"' (*EG*, nos 14,15).

This first reflection on human being-in-the-world as a fundamental perspective of theological anthropology can be formulated thus: faith is the transcendental way of being-in-the-world of people who understand history, who open themselves to an enriching being-with [*Mit-Sein*] other human beings, and at the same time is the satisfying vital energy of human beings, and is guaranteed by God. It is an energy that makes an individual's life, and the life of others (his or hers and their being-in-the-world) a satisfying and joyful life.

After this first reflection we now turn our attention to human corporeality. In philosophical anthropology, this is regarded as the second decisive essential datum.

CHAPTER 3
# THE SECOND FUNDAMENTAL CHARACTERISTIC OF MODERN ANTHROPOLOGY: CORPOREALITY

*1. The philosophical characterization of corporeality*

Gabriel Amengual dedicated a chapter in his philosophical anthropology to an analysis of human corporeality or embodiment – in his publication he speaks of *corporalidad*. It is precisely in this area that a very tangible radical change has occurred that has profoundly marked the image of the human being. In the first part, Amengual makes use of a number of empirical enquiries. A massive number of these had been set in motion already in the nineteenth century, following philosophical reflections that were the basis for these enquiries. From the beginning of the twentieth century until today they have contributed hugely to clarifying the history of human development within the context of the general theory of evolution.

In this first part, the author deals with the human body as a 'physical body', meaning as the result of the grand process of cosmic development. Then follows a section on the 'living body', which from a biological point of view is placed within a range of bodies of living beings which are the object of development. As it proceeds, periods and characteristics of such development are given. Then follow particular topics, for example, upright movement, formation of the hand, development of the brain. The author is careful each time to link these with related steps in the development of human culture. Finally, he deals with the 'limitations' of the human being compared to animals. These limitations are already given by the phenomenon of the 'physiologically precocious birth' of the human being, since from this birth comes the need – especially at the biological level – to learn in order to be able to survive. The conclusion is a paragraph on evolutionism and in general on the question of faith in creation and the different epistemic approaches that derive from it. Then, corresponding to this data comes another reflection on the beginnings of human life.

In the sections that follow, this well-documented scientific overview is systematically developed from a philosophical perspective. At the beginning of this second section, which is even longer than the preceding one, Amengual offers a sketch of pre-philosophical anthropology which he illustrates by reference to the Bible and Homer. The author outlines the persistent influence of the Stoic and Platonic notions of the human being which – in the field of theological anthropology – then lead to the pre-corporeal existence of the soul[1] and especially to existence after death. Linked to this is the devaluation of the body, to the benefit of spiritual existence and the existence of the soul.

The Church's proclamation, and especially the development of the *eschata* in the history of theology, but

---

1 Cf. for example, reflections by Origen.

also spirituality and the spiritual practice of faith of the Catholic Church, were profoundly affected by this. A summary description of the Aristotelian and Thomistic understanding clearly shows the differences compared to the Stoic and Platonic tradition, without ignoring what has been kept of this dualistic notion. Along with a new view of the embodiment of human existence, fundamental for the unfolding of modernity, is the inclusion of human self-experience in philosophy through phenomenology. The first effects clearly show up in Hegel's philosophy of law. From this, Amengual draws the fundamental formulations that have guided him in his understanding of corporeality, which he then documents abundantly with individual contributions drawn from the history of philosophy. In his *Elements of the Philosophy of Right*, Hegel states that man is his body and at the same time possesses his body. It is a famous formula which Plessner takes up again in his anthropology, making it his central claim. Hegel says:

> As a person, I am myself an immediate individual; if we give further precision to this expression, it means in the first instance that I am alive in this bodily organism which is my external existence, universal in content and undivided, the real pre-condition of every further determined mode of existence. But, all the same, as person, I possess my life and my body, like other things, only in so far as my will is in them ... I possess the members of my body, my life, only so long as I

will to possess them. An animal cannot maim or destroy itself, but a man can.[2]

By way of explanation, Hegel adds, in §48:

> In so far as the body is an immediate existent, it is not in conformity with mind. If it is to be the willing organ and soul-endowed instrument of the mind, it must first be taken into possession by mind (see §57). But from the point of view of others, I am in essence a free entity in my body while my possession of it is still immediate.
>
> It is only because I am alive as a free entity in my body that this living existent ought not to be misused by being made a beast of burden. While I am alive, my soul (the concept and, to use a higher term, the free entity) and my body are not separated; my body is the embodiment of my freedom and it is with my body that I feel. It is therefore only abstract sophisticated reasoning which can so distinguish body and soul as to hold that the 'thing-in-itself', the soul, is not touched or attacked if the body is maltreated and the existent embodiment of personality is subjected to the power of another.

---

2 Quoted from GWF HEGEL, *Elements of the Philosophy of Right*, First Published: by G. Bell, London, 1896. Translated: by S. W. Dyde, 1896. Preface and Introduction with certain changes in terminology: from "Philosophy of Right", by G W F HEGEL 1820, Translated. Prometheus Books; Remainder: from "Hegel's Philosophy of Right", 1820, translated, Oxford University Press; First Published: by Clarendon Press 1952, Translated: with Notes by T. M. Knox 1942., §47, §48.

> I can withdraw into myself out of my bodily existence and make my body something external to myself; particular feelings I can regard as something outside me and in chains I can still be free. But this is my will; so far as others are concerned, I am in my body. To be free from the point of view of others is identical with being free in my determined existence. If another does violence to my body, he does violence to me.
>
> If my body is touched or suffers violence, then, because I feel, I am touched myself actually, here and now. This creates the distinction between personal injury and damage to my external property, for in such property my will is not actually present in this direct fashion.

I have included this lengthy quotation because the author explains himself on the basis of these classic characteristics of human bodily existence, already formulated by Hegel, as well as using other philosophies and phenomenologies as his basis. With the expression 'taking possession of the body', Amengual rightly intends the formation, cultivation, education and personalization of human existence, the free translation in real and actual terms that happens with the ego's being a body.[3] For the human being in particular, the body establishes the place where he is in space. Starting from corporeal existence, the dimensions of space are then developed. The human being can only exist in certain spaces thanks to the body, that body that the person is, which makes

---

3   Cf. G AMENGUAL. *Antropologia filosofica, cit., 83 ff.*

it possible for the person to be-there in the world. The body determines perspective and horizon, establishes the concrete presence of the person, so the person can be there for others, can use and profit from what is other, can inhabit the world and know how to belong to the world.

The conclusion to these reflections on corporeality is made up of the specifics of being a man and being a woman as ways of being human, as essential ways of being a person, and includes communication in general, etc. As a result of deep reflection, the author describes how sexuality – as the vital force and creator of relationships – possesses its subject in freedom and in the body; how from there its integration and dominance by the human being can interrelate. By way of a summary, the author then once again mentions the significance of the human body, first of all as a means by which human beings can express themselves and their limitations; as a means of being present in a significant way for others as being present [*Gegenwärtiger*] in the world, as a place of communication and encounter and in relationship with the given human and material world; and in relationship with inner structures and ways of being.

## 2.  Observations on 'corporeality' in the context of papal magisterial documents

This very much simplified sketch of the concept of corporeality demonstrates the extreme complexity of theological anthropology. The change is huge when compared with medieval and late medieval theological anthropology, and particularly so when compared with the Baroque scholastic period, and the theology of the Enlightenment and Neo-scholastic periods.

Questions have been opened up which have not as yet been taken up in systematic theology. Hence, given the way in which we have posed the question, we cannot infer that Pope Francis, in the context of his papal magisterial documents, has dealt with all possible aspects and details of this chapter of a study which is still to be written on corporeality in the context of theological anthropology. Nevertheless, we find some texts in his magisterial documents which most decidedly enter into the theme of corporeality within today's theological anthropology.

By way of illustration, let us take Pope Francis' Encyclical *Laudato Si'* (*LS*) on caring for our common home, issued on 24 May 2015, the Solemnity of Pentecost.

Where does a modern theological anthropology show up in this Encyclical, especially where corporeality is concerned? If readers turn to the handful of Pope Francis' introductory notes, they will find some words of Saint Francis of Assisi quoted at the beginning of the Encyclical:

> "LAUDATO SI', mi' Signore" – "Praise be to you, my Lord". In the words of this beautiful canticle, Saint Francis of Assisi reminds us that our common home is like a sister with whom we share our life and a beautiful mother who opens her arms to embrace us. "Praise be to you, my Lord, through our Sister, Mother Earth, who sustains and governs us, and who produces various fruit with coloured flowers and herbs."

> This sister now cries out to us because of the harm we have inflicted on her by our irresponsible use and abuse of the goods with which God has endowed her. We have come to see ourselves as her lords and masters, entitled to plunder her at will. The violence present in our hearts, wounded by sin, is also reflected in the symptoms of sickness evident in the soil, in the water, in the air and in all forms of life. This is why the earth herself, burdened and laid waste, is among the most abandoned and maltreated of our poor; she "groans in travail" (Rom 8:22). We have forgotten that we ourselves are dust of the earth (cf. Gen 2:7); our very bodies are made up of her elements, we breathe her air and we receive life and refreshment from her waters. (*LS*, no. 2).

The images and expressions used to sing about planet earth, our common home, are taken in general from the sphere of human embodiment. The earth becomes a sister, a *personified* sister with whom we share life. There is a description of the 'mother who opens her arms to embrace us' and who produces various fruits and nourishes us.

This sister 'now cries out to us' due to the harm caused by our irresponsible use and abuse of her goods. In the symptoms of her illness – and this image too, deals with human embodiment – the 'violence present in our hearts, wounded by sin' is reflected. She is described in terms of the earth, which 'groans in travail.' The introductory section concludes with the words: 'our very bodies are made up of her elements, we breathe her air and we receive life and refreshment from her waters.'

This language is not simply a harmonious metaphor which can be used as an inviting way of speaking in an introductory text. The words 'sister' or 'mother earth', the bodily relationship with everything, the human, bodily, individual and social set of relationships with everything run through various chapters, whether speaking of the various kinds of environmental pollution, or of climate change, water problems, loss of genetic diversity or the worsening quality of life and social injustices. These key words are also a feature of questions regarding the human roots of the ecological crisis, where it speaks of technology and the technocratic paradigm, of modern anthropocentrism or of biological innovations resulting from research. Last but not least, these words are the tracks on which the fundamental features of 'ecological education and spirituality', which the Pope speaks about, are developed. At the beginning of the section on ecological education and spirituality, Pope Francis writes: 'We lack an awareness of our common origin, of our mutual belonging, and of a future to be shared with everyone. This basic awareness would enable the development of new convictions, attitudes and forms of life. A great cultural, spiritual and educational challenge stands before us, and it will demand that we set out on the long path of renewal' (*LS*, no. 202).

The challenge is described especially as one of overcoming a 'utilitarian mindset' (*LS*, no. 210) and the myths of modernity based on it: individualism, unlimited progress, competition, consumerism, the unregulated market (*LS*, no. 210). Pope Francis speaks explicitly of the need to develop new laws, noting at the same time that laws cannot be imposed unless the majority of members of society accept them voluntarily and consciously. What is essential is an overall change of lifestyle, of daily habits in a wide range of dimensions and contexts of human existence.

However, this means that the fundamental characteristics described as part of human embodiment must be taken up in a genuine and grateful human way: the pure gift, freely given, of bodily existence in the world; respect for this gift despite its essential limitations in how it is used, and the recognition and protection of this precious gift.

These are the essential features of corporeality that emerge in human terms in Francis' Christian message when he speaks of 'Sister' and 'Mother Earth'. This song expresses the truth, not an enthusiasm based solely on feelings.

Thus the Pope deals with the need for a revision and conversion understood in a theological and Christian sense, since here it is Christians who have sinned against creation in so many ways, have mistreated and humiliated it, tormented it. Human corporeality does not simple describe something that subsists, a *res extensa* – as Descartes says – or any kind of object. The corporeal modes of human existence, of basic openness, of the most varied relationships with others and for others, precede all the other modes of the presence [*Gegenwärtigkeit*] of relationships between entities, are their foundation, and hence do not replace them but give them their place and meaning.

If we compare Pope Francis' arguments in the Encyclical *LS* with, for example, the report by the Science Council of the German Federal Government [*Globale Umweltveränderungen, Welt im Wandel, Gesellschaftsvertrag für eine große Transformation*, Global Environmental Change, World in Transition, Social Contract for a Great Transformation (Berlin 2011)], a clear difference emerges.

The report for the German Government obviously includes a presentation in the area of the natural sciences of the processes responsible for climate change, and does so with scientific urgency. However, it also points to the social, economic and political challenges tied up with the new situation which, on the basis of experience, are connected with a huge transformation of the kind that took place at the beginning of the process of settlement, etc. It clearly emerges that in this new situation a transformation of social processes and life habits is necessary. An impressive picture emerges from all this information of the ethical and moral but also political challenges. The result is a picture of the very difficult processes to be undertaken for the formation of a social awareness essential for humanity and its future.

By contrast, based on its theological approach, the Encyclical offers the vision of a *meaningful context of reality* that encapsulates the marked scientific, technical, and economic changes, but anchors all of these statements in a larger overall horizon opened up by faith and – in a critical comparison – makes them acceptable and places them within the context of the history of salvation. A new theological image of the human being is outlined here, one which is decidedly different from earlier Christian images of the human being. Likewise, there is a new vision of evil, sin and its destructive, life-negating power in modern life. Here, however, a certain weakness shows up in the reasoning process in Pope Francis' Encyclical. It is a shortcoming in reasoning stemming from the fact that a corresponding theological analysis of scientific and philosophical anthropology and its insights has so far not been carried out with necessary emphasis by Catholic theology. This observation refers in particular to the complex of questions and insights that have emerged over the past 150 years with regard to human corporeality: the selfsameness [*Selbigkeit*] of body and soul, the adoption of a substance metaphysics for the purpose of defining human beings, the human beings place in the evolutionary process, etc.

What emerges from this omission on the part of theology and theologians? The Pope, in his teaching, essentially refers to the strong spiritual teachings of Francis in order to present the view of faith on today's problem. He mixes the central propositions of modern anthropology with this view of faith and compares them with a realistic analysis of today's crisis. But in doing this, he cannot rely on broader, already existing theological developments of theological anthropology. The consequence is that for a considerable number of scientists and business leaders, responsible technicians and sociologists, the foundations of this spiritual and religious viewpoint seem to be barely reconcilable with their 'knowledge of the facts' and their judgement on the general situation.

Their question is: is Francis' stance not 'merely' one of metaphorical and religious over-enthusiasm, at least for our times? Of course, in itself, his way of speaking is extremely interesting, but it comes out of a medieval horizon of experience. After all, such a view corresponded to the medieval view of the cosmos, which was characterized by a theistic, metaphysical, philosophical order of thinking. There are not many environmental researchers who, like Ulrich von Weizsäcker,[4] discover the much larger, more comprehensive framework that Pope Francis prescribes here. Comprehensive not only for publications such as the above-mentioned memorandum for the Federal Government, but also once again compared to the teaching of previous pontificates, which are essentially limited to hopeful statements.[5]

*3. Observations on the phenomenon of corporeality in the post-synodal document,* Amoris Laetitia

The Encyclical *LS* deals with a number of individual questions of philosophical and theological anthropology, above all those keywords that Gabriel Amengual subscribes to and summarizes in the fundamentals of corporeality,

---

4  Cf. W GEORGE (ed.) *Laudato Si' – Wissenschaftler antworten auf die Enzyklika von Papst Franziskus,* Gießen 2017. See especially the presentation by Ernst Ulrich von Weiszäcker (9 ff.); an example of the critique often made by scholars of economics and represented by M. Becker, *Ein Lesebericht aus wirtschaftswissenschaftlicher Perspektive* pp. 129-148.
5  Cf. PAUL VI, Apostolic Exhortation *Octogesima Adveniens;* JOHN PAUL II, Encyclical *Redemptor Hominis, ID.,* Encyclical *Centesimus Annus;* BENEDICT XVI, Encyclical *Caritas in Veritate.*

for example, under the notion of human destiny. This is true especially in the chapter on *Actividad*,[6] activity, with paragraphs headed: Action, Poiesis and Practice; Work-Technique, Leisure; Culture-Nature-Technology; Diversity of Cultures and Traditions, Construction of Society, and Solidarity. So we turned to the theological framework of the Encyclical and to its 'anthropological platform', so to speak, because there 'corporeality' is addressed as a basic phenomenon.

The post-synodal document *Amoris Laetitia*, on the other hand, substantially supplements the view of theological anthropology insofar as in its biblical part this document offers a most impressive interpretation of the history of the creation of the human being and outlines the New Testament statements deriving from it. In both respects 'corporeality' plays a key role as the basic trait of being human.

Pope Francis begins his exposition of marriage and the family in the Bible with the sentence: 'The Bible is full of families, births, love stories and family crises. This is true from its very first page, with the appearance of Adam and Eve's family with all its burden of violence but also its enduring strength (cf. Gen 4) to its very last page, where we behold the wedding feast of the Bride and the Lamb (Rev 21:2, 9).'[7] To the question on 'the human couple in its deepest reality' (*AL*, no. 10), Francis replies by referring to Jesus who quotes Gen 1:27: 'God created man in his own image, in the

6 Cf. G AMENGUAL, *Antropología filosófica, cit., 279 ff.*

7 FRANCIS, post-synodal Apostolic Exhortation *Amoris Laetitia,* 19 March 2016, no. 8.

image of God he created them; male and female he created them.' The 'male and female he created them' is picked out to explain the idea that man is in the image of God. The Pope interprets it in a way that is alien to traditional exegesis from the Patristic era: 'The couple that loves and begets life is a true, living icon – not an idol like those of stone or gold prohibited by the Decalogue – capable of revealing God the Creator and Saviour. For this reason, fruitful love becomes a symbol of God's inner life' (*AL*, no. 11). The Pope reinforces this new approach with an exegetical note: '… The ability of human couples to beget life is the path along which the history of salvation progresses' (*ivi*). As testimony to this is the 'priestly tradition' 'interwoven with various genealogical accounts.' 'The couple's fruitful relationship becomes an image for understanding and describing the mystery of God himself,' to which the Christian vision of the Trinity corresponds. The Trinity is not solitude bu a communion of love. Thus, the original, corporeal behaviour in life of the 'loving couple' is characterized as a place and initial experiential context for the presence of God and the self as well as for the world's experience of the human being.

In close correspondence with this, Pope Francis interprets the creation of the woman in the second creation report (Gen 2:18-2, 22). The Pope speaks of 'the man, who anxiously seeks "a helper fit for him."' Along with Levínas, Francis speaks of the encounter of Adam with 'a face, a "thou", who reflects God's own love and is man's "best possession, a helper fit for him and a pillar of support", in the words of the biblical sage (Sir 36:24).' 'This encounter, which relieves man's solitude, gives rise to new birth and to the family.' Both, man and woman, are joined 'in a closeness both physical and interior, to such an extent that the word is used to describe our union with God' (*AL*, no. 13). 'The result of this union is that the two "become one flesh", both physically and in the union of their hearts and lives, and, eventually, in a child, who will share not only genetically but also spiritually in the "flesh" of both parents' (*ivi*).

Francis himself considers the changed interpretative horizon of his exegesis when he says: 'Adam, who is also the man of every time and place, together with his wife, starts a new family ... and the two shall become one." It is a 'primordial event' of an historical and transcendental kind in which God is fully immersed and in which the beginning of history as history takes place in the body.

The originality and autonomy of this interpretation of Genesis can only be understood if one understands modern philosophical anthropology as Amengual has characterized it, for example in his discussion of 'corporeality'.

Gen 1:1 corresponds to the 'givennness' of the world, to the givenness of everything, of 'heaven and earth', as given by the nameless divinity.

Gen 1:2-31 represents everything that exists in the 'world', including human beings.

Gen 1:26-31 speaks of the human being in his or her peculiarity and difference from all other things: the beginning of the world and the beginning of history in its corporeal existence as man and woman. At the same time, this highlights the fundamental difference between the human being, man and woman, and the rest of the world: the world and everything in it is 'other' to the human being, the place of residence, the habitat, and serves human beings, but they live essentially from this other and are dependent on it.

Philosophical anthropology shows how time and space are constituted by means of corporeality. In bodily perception, the temporal-spatial world opens up.[8]

With regard to being man or woman, Amengual sums up:

> Sexuality refers to gender difference, male and female, which involves mutual attraction, the reproductive function of the genus, psychological differences in character, and cultural and social characteristics. The relationship of both sexes is implied in their difference. The human meaning of sexual difference is rooted essentially in the relationship between persons, that is, in the mutuality of the encounter between personal, incarnated beings, in such a way as to assert that the relationship itself and its fulfilment in love reveal the nature of sexuality. In this sense, sexuality is not just a dimension of one's own body, but also our relationships with others.[9]

It is this summary of phenomenological research which forms the background to the interpretation of Pope Francis'

---

8 In this context, Gabriel Amengual makes particular reference to Merleau-Ponty and Ortega and Gasset. (cf. G AMENGUAL. *Antropología filosófica, cit., 83-85*), but also to analyses that followed by Paul Ricoeur, Bernhard Waldenfels, etc. ...

9 *Ibidem*, 87.

second creation account in *Amorsi Laetitia*.[10] There is not a 'reconstruction' of a philosophical presupposition in an entirely different dimension, not a 'replica' on the basis of one blueprint. Rather, it is a consistent understanding of the basic 'responsive'[11] structures of human corporeality as the mode of human existence on the one hand, and on the other, of perception and faith.

When they become one 'flesh', one 'heart and soul', the bonds that govern here are of a physical and inner nature, but we cannot easily describe them either in the philosophical or in the theological field as metaphysical causes of an activity of an accidental type defined in categories. It is a common accomplishment and fulfilment of life which is addressed.

---

10  Cf. above, p. 50.
11  This is the term used by Bernhard Waldenfels, a disciple of Merleau-Ponty and Paul Ricoeur, in *Antwortregister, Frankfurt 1994.*

CHAPTER 4
# THE BASIC TRAITS OF 'CORPOREALITY' IN THE HUMAN BEING: AFFECTIVITY, LANGUAGE, SPIRIT AND PERSON IN HUMAN BEING-THERE [*DA-SEIN*]

*1. Affectivity as a basic way of being human*

a) Affectivity [*Befindlichkeit*]: its philosophical rediscovery.

With the new discoveries of phenomenology at the beginning of the twentieth century, a new discovery began of the emotional world, the mind, the senses, of affectivity. While Kant notes in his *Anthropology from a Pragmatic point of View*: 'By the way, affect, considered by itself alone, is always imprudent; it makes itself incapable of pursuing its own end, and it is therefore unwise to allow it to come into being intentionally'[1] at the same time he praises apathy and maintains that the passions 'do the greatest harm to freedom; and if emotion is *drunkenness*, passion is an *illness* that abhors all medicine.'[2] Instead, with his great works, *The Nature of Sympathy*, and *Formalism in Ethics and Non-formal Ethics of Values: A New Attempt Toward the Foundation of an Ethical Personalism*, Max Scheler began a new basic

1 I. Kant, *Anthropology from a Pragmatic Point of View*. (Ed.) Robert B Louden, with an introduction by Manfred Kuehn, Cambridge University Press 2006, p. 151.
2 *Ibidem*, p. 266

reflection on affectivity, feelings, passions etc. In Heidegger's *Being and Time*, the 'mental state [*Befindlichkeit*]' or 'the temperamental tone [*Gestimmt-sein*]' of the human being is part of the 'existential constitution' of human existence on which the understanding and fundamental interpretation of existence in the world is based.[3]

Paul Ricoeur has made significant contributions to the analysis of affectivity in his 1950 study: *Freedom and nature: The Voluntary and the Involuntary* and his famous work: *Fallible Man*, Paris 1960, especially in the section on the 'Fragility of the Affective.'[4]

Gabriel Amengual did not explore these differentiated questions and concepts of Ricoeur in his *Antropología filosófica* – ideas that extended as far as his final works, for example *Oneself as Another*, regarding the self and identity – but established his interpretation of affectivity by referring to Ortega y Gasset and Josef Pieper's work on love. He shows here how on the one hand love is rooted in affectivity and can never be separated from this root, while at the same time is the fulfilment of this fundamental human encounter with reality.

b) The significance of affectivity in Pope Francis' theological anthropology.

Pope Francis deals more insistently with the questions of affectivity in the post-synodal document *Amoris Laetitia*

---

3   Cf. M Heidegger, *Being and Time*, cit., §29.
4   Cf. P Ricoeur, *Fallible Man*, trans. Charles A. Kelbley, with an introduction by Walter J. Lowe, New York: Fordham University Press, 1986 (1960).

(*AL*). At the beginning of his chapter on love in marriage, he offers a very precise exegetical interpretation of the Song of Songs and love in St Paul's First Letter to the Corinthians. Here he focuses very much on individual verbs by which love is characterized, and the negations found there. This way, the whole gamut of affectivity is clearly outlined, but no less so also the fragility and risks involved in real forms of loving.

In the section that follows, the Pope describes conjugal love as it moves through its various stages, first of all as friendship (*caritas*) that seeks the good of the other for their own sake. Then in the concluding section he tackles the erotic dimension of marriage, especially as the root and basis for openness to the other. In one comment, Francis refers expressly to Thomas Aquinas, who in the first part of the *Summa* poses the question of whether God is needed for there to be love as *amor*. The answer is that: '*Primus motus voluntatis et cuiuslibet appetitae virtutis est amor*' (Love is the first movement of the will and of every appetitive faculty). So the whole 'world of emotions' belongs to love (*AL*, nos 143-146) and the associated 'pleasure' of God's children, but also the fragility and dangers of love due to violence and manipulation, since the power of 'reaching out' and 'attraction' is in need of cultural development and mediation in order to develop all of its meaning and significance.

The profound meaning of the inclusion of *eros* within marriage, without in any way reducing it, is shown in the description of the sacrament of marriage as a divine vocation of two human beings who enter mutually into a covenant for life so that they belong to one another as steadfastly and wholeheartedly as Christ and the Church belong to one another. They receive the promise of divine assistance for this covenant of life which finds itself so much at risk.

Pope Francis' familiarity with modern research on affectivity is found not only in *AL*, though. In his reflections on social issues, Francis similarly takes up positive analyses of human instincts like possession (property, money, etc.), wealth (power, domination), and things that count (honour, dignity). All of these instincts can only be preserved over time through cultural development and by mediating their ever threatening transformation into institutional distortions and forms of human oppression. There are no general ideal forms for these cultural developments and mediations, which always vary in space and time, that could be implemented in a straightforward manner. There are only relative 'improvements' conditioned by time – and place. Paul Ricoeur has offered the necessary philosophical and phenomenological analyses.[5]

## 2. On the linguistics of human existence

a) Language and linguistics as a primary field of research in modern philosophy.

While language was considered in scholarly philosophical linguistic usage of the 17th and 18th centuries to be an "expression of thought through arbitrarily chosen signs,"[6]

5 Cf. P. Ricoeur, *Die Fehlbarkeit*, (Fallible Man) cit., 164-172.
6 Cf. J Hennigfeld, *Sprache – Philosophisch*, in *RGG* 4, 7, 1608.

at the turn of the 19th century, philosophical reflection on language brings it to the forefront of philosophizing in modern times. At the same time, linguistics is undergoing such a transformation that it is only possible to present a sketch here of this new-found reality. In the context given here, it is merely a matter of listing key words and names in order to show how linguistic thinking in modern times is considered as a way of being human. The dependence of reason on language is vigorously emphasized already in critiques by Hamann and Herder and up to Kant, such that from there on Kant's 'pure reason' is radically being questioned. Wilhelm von Humboldt then traced out new approaches to an understanding of language.[7] Worthy of mention at the turn of the twentieth century are the Viennese Carnap, Fleger and Russel and especially Wittgenstein and his *Philosophical Investigations*.

A contemporary of Wittgenstein's,[8] that is at the time of the First World War, Franz Rosenzweig worked on his *Star*

---

7  The titles clearly indicate the emerging innovations: *On the Comparative Study of Language and its Relation to the Different Periods of Language Development* (1820); *On the Diversity of Human Language Construction and Its Influence on the Mental Development of the Human Species*; *On the Origin of Grammatical Forms and their Influence on the Development of Ideas* (1822); *The national character of languages (fragment); Alphabetic writing and its relationship to the structure of language* (1824); *The dual* (1827); *On the Diversity of Human Language Construction and its Influence on the Mental Development of the Human Species* (1830-1835), A Flitner – K Diel (Hg.), Wilhelm von Humboldt Werke, Vol. 3, *Schriften zur Sprachphilosophie*, Darmstadt 1963.

8  Cf. *Ludwig Wittgenstein 1914-1916*, Wilhelm Baum (ed.), Vienna-Berlin 1991

*of Redemption*, the development of a 'new way of thinking' which is based on biblical language, especially the liturgy. He joined Cohen and worked with Martin Buber on the German Bible translation.

Along with Scheler it is essential to name Heidegger and his pupils, such as Gadamer. Heidegger notes in *Being and Time* that speech belongs to 'the intrinsic summary' of existence and is part of its disclosure [*Erschlossenbeit*].[9] In the second half of the twentieth century, in criticism and as a continuation of earlier approaches, a plethora of language functions are presented and reflected on. Consider, for example, speech act theory. There is structural linguistics, which undertakes to decode the history of thought by starting from language and linguistics, and power structures are examined in terms of linguistic philosophy. Moral normativity develops from discourse ethics. Add to these few selective key words the profound changes in linguistics which have not even been mentioned here.

The question arises: is this unprecedented abundance of new insights, contexts, different approaches in theological anthropology reflected in Pope Francis' magisterial documents?

b) Observations on the theological understanding of human linguistics in *Evangelii Gaudium*.

To respond to these questions, it is advisable to refer to the Apostolic Exhortation *Evangelii Gaudium* (*EG*) by Pope

---

9   M Heidegger, *Being and Time*, (p. 169 in German edition).

Francis. The third chapter bears the title: The Proclamation of the Gospel. Its four subsections are:

1. The entire people of God proclaims the Gospel
2. The homily
3. Preparing to preach
4. Evangelization and the deeper understanding of the kerygma.

These headings already testify to how the question of language – from very different perspectives – is being explored in a theological context.

In what follows we break our observations down on the basis of these four subtitles. We will be guided overall by the heading of the entire chapter: The Proclamation of the Gospel.

In *Lumen Fidei* (*LF*) and in the introduction to *EG*, he has already spoken of the Word of God addressed to every human being and finding a response in faith.[10] For this he refers to *Dei Verbum* (*DV*), the Constitution on Revelation, especially the arguments of the first chapter on revelation itself, through which God made himself known to our first parents (cf. *DV*, nos 2-3). This fundamental statement was already discussed above in the section on man's being-in-the-world. In the third chapter of *EG* it is about the proclamation of the Gospel and the first basic statement is that 'The entire people of God proclaims the Gospel' (*EG*, the title of the first subsection of the third chapter).

---

10   Cf. above, p. 29 ff.

Language is always the language of a people, and this 'people' can initially be the community of disciples on the day of Pentecost: the message of the gospel can only be proclaimed if the Spirit seizes the disciples as a whole, and the language of evangelization is born. This language of proclamation presumes that there is already the language of the Old Testament.

The language of proclamation is the expression of faith and thus constitutes the community of believers, the Church as Church. It is addressed to everyone, is not a particular, separate language, meaning an elite language. And it is essentially an action, an evangelizing action. It is not just expressed through the life of the community of believers, and it cannot be, must not be transmitted simply as information. In pragmatic terms it is an address which includes all the people. In this way, both non-thematic statements, meaning corporeal and social attestations of the gospel, and intentionally thematic statements are equally part of this proclamation. 'No one is saved by himself or herself, individually, or by his or her own efforts. God attracts us by taking into account the complex interweaving of personal relationships entailed in the life of a human community. This people which God has chosen and called is the Church' (*EG*, no. 113).

At the beginning of his remarks on the homily, Francis says: 'Let us renew our confidence in preaching, based on the conviction that it is God who seeks to reach out to others through the preacher, and that he displays his power through human words. Saint Paul speaks forcefully about the need to preach, since the Lord desires to reach other people by means of our word' (*EG*, no. 136).

The oft-quoted words of the Swiss reformer Heinrich Bullinger: '*Praedicatio verbi Dei est verbum Dei*' (The preaching of the Word of God is the Word of God) are thus transformed from an assertion into a sentence of faith and trust that leaves the free initiative to God. The statement is at the same time protected from accusations from the more recent controversy on monotheism.[11] The Pope refers to the preaching of Jesus, the statements of Paul on the need for preaching and the sending of the disciples and the preaching of the apostles. The homily as the 'liturgical proclamation of the Word of God especially in the Eucharistic assembly' is the highest form of this communication: the conversation of God with his people, one in which the wonders of salvation are proclaimed and the demands of the covenant are constantly brought to mind.

The homily gains its character from being anchored in the liturgy which is the memorial of Jesus Christ, his proclamation, his gift of self in the Passion and his being glorified by the Father, and his sacramental communion which transforms the lives of believers. It follows, then, that:

1. It should be short, respecting the balance of the elements and rhythm of the liturgy. It should lead to Jesus Christ himself.

---

11   For an interpretation of this notion of preaching, cf. K BARTH, *Die kirchliche Dogmatik*, Vol 1, *Die Lebre vom Wert Gottes*, I/1, 52, 56ff, 71ff. There is fundamental agreement between Barth and Francis, apart from a few details.

2. Because the homily is intended to foster an intimate conversation between God and believers, the preacher should express himself in authentic language and 'find in the heart of people and their culture a source of living water, which helps the preacher to know what must be said and how to say it' (*EG*, no. 139).

3, Finally, the preacher must be familiar with Scripture, with the message. Francis sums this up with the image of a conversation between a mother and her child: 'The spirit of love which reigns in a family guides both mother and child in their conversations; therein they teach and learn, experience correction and grow in appreciation of what is good. Something similar happens in a homily' (*EG*, no. 139).

The remarks on the preparation of the homily – subdivided into sections: 'Reverence for truth', 'Personalizing the word', 'Spiritual reading', 'An ear to the people', 'homiletic resources' – read like an introduction to an effective and responsible approach and an associated authentic way of life so that the preacher avoids slipping into chitchat, meaningless prattle, and a style that seems to leave out any reference to self, the other and the topic being spoken about. Only in this way can beauty and goodness accompany the truth of language.

The chapter concludes with some remarks on catechesis. Pope Francis makes a careful distinction between kerygma and evangelization or catechesis. Kerygma points to the innermost mystery of Christian language. The Pope also calls kerygma first announcement, thus describing its nature as an event. He does not define it, because it cannot be defined. Instead, he describes it with a metaphor drawn from the New Testament:

> The fire of the Spirit is given in the form of tongues and leads us to believe in Jesus Christ who, by his death and resurrection, reveals and communicates to us the Father's infinite mercy. On the lips of the catechist the first proclamation must ring out over and over: "Jesus Christ loves you; he gave his life to save you; and now he is living at your side every day to enlighten, strengthen and free you." This first proclamation is called "first" not because it exists at the beginning and can then be forgotten or replaced by other more important things. It is first in a qualitative sense because it is the principal proclamation, the one which we must hear again and again in different ways, the one which we must announce one way or another throughout the process of catechesis, at every level and moment (*EG*, no. 164).[1]

Catechesis about the kerygma is to be distinguished from kerygma. The former cannot replace the latter and

---

1  In my opinion, Bruno Forte has presented what is taught here in terms of a systematic theology approach: 'The kerygma can be described as an authoritative proclamation of the saving event that God worked in Jesus Christ. In him, this event is realized in the power of the Holy Spirit through the words of the Church's proclamation, and reaches the listener in a personal way charged with such meaning that the proclamation draws the listener's attention to the message and helps him or her to come to the decision for Christ' (B FORTE, *Kerygma II systematisch-theologisch*, in *LtbK* 5, 1409).

does not give way to a 'more solid' formation (*EG*, no. 165). Rather does it accompany and mediate growth in faith: this not only means entering more deeply into the teachings of the faith, but a practical expression of new life mediated by the kerygma. Such a catechesis articulates God's redeeming love to which the human being must correspond with moral and ethical actions.

Francis expressly mentions 'mystagogical' catechesis as the second form of catechesis. It explains the Church's sacramental or liturgical signs and thus presents the solemn form of practically shaping Church language. In this context, Francis notes specifically that every form of catechesis should pay attention to 'the way of beauty' (via *pulchritudinis*). 'We must be bold enough to discover new signs and new symbols, new flesh to embody and communicate the word, and different forms of beauty which are valued in different cultural settings, including those unconventional modes of beauty which may mean little to the evangelizers, yet prove particularly attractive for others' (*EG*, no. 167).

Francis adds a final paragraph to these two kinds of catechesis on 'personal accompaniment in the processes of growth'. Spiritual accompaniment seems to be especially necessary in modern times to help believers gain 'true freedom' in today's world. This spiritual accompaniment serves to 'awaken a yearning for the Christian ideal: the desire to respond fully to God's love and to bring to fruition what he has sown in our lives' (*EG*, no. 171). Today this is an essential part of the Church's proclamation. In the same way, the offer of shared scripture reading serves the common growth and deepening of the faith.

## 3. Man: spirit and personhood

a) Consciousness: spirit and personhood in the human being according to modern philosophy.

The author introduces his philosophical approach to the 'spirit of man' with the question of consciousness. Along the lines of J.R. Searle's work in 2001, *Mente, lenguaje y sociedad*, and Anthony Kenny's *Metaphysics of Mind*, by *espíritu*, Amengual means spirit in the sense of *mens*. Mens indicates the human being's ability to develop intellectual behaviours. Because the concept of person is directly related to the phenomenon of the mind, in this section we summarize both.

First of all, applying careful phenomenological analysis, the author clarifies what is meant by consciousness and self-consciousness. Consciousness is initially a consciousness of something. It cannot be defined: it simply is. It is only from here that one has the opportunity to experience something as experience and to pay attention to that experience, to intend experience itself. In such coming-to-know, it becomes apparent that all states of consciousness belong to an actor - in the first person, an ego. This opens up the 'externality' and 'inwardness' of experience. Consciousness emerges as a unity of subject and object, an insight that contradicts 'normal, everyday ideas' as well as scientifically widespread interpretations. In his analysis the author follows the logic which Georg Friedrich Wilhelm Hegel presents in the fourth chapter of his *Phenomenology of Spirit*.[2]

Consciousness involves diachronous and synchronous unity: this unity refers to all facts in the sequence of memory which at the same time belong to consciousness. We can distinguish different states of consciousness in this unity. They belong in a context and have their identity and characteristics in a network of states of consciousness. The states of consciousness and their network, however, are experienced by 'me'. Although they can be 'objectively examined,' they are merely 'subjective,' and they are each experienced as singular facts.

Emerging here are the relationships to the modes of existence of the human being, which are dealt with under the key term 'affectivity'. In this sense, every single person lives and moves in his or her world. Every new state of consciousness is integrated into the existing network and experiences its identity and singularity in contrast to the other states of consciousness. In this sense it is true that every single person moves within in his or her world, lives in it.

But it is also true that in the encounter with the other, each ones consciousness gives access to a world that is different from their own world. In behaviour towards the other and to many others, questions about the other worlds and their facts emerge – questions of a cognitive kind – and questions of the will regarding change, use, influence, etc.

---

2 Cf. GWF Hegel, *The Phenomenology of Spirit*, tr. A. V. Miller, OUP 1977, 'The truth of self-certainty' p. 104.

In this context individual 'consciousness' comes about, as G. Mead's analysis has indicated.[3]

The native and radical ability to develop the specifically human possibilities and attitudes that are needed here are called '*mens*' in the tradition. The term describes the extremely complex ability to produce linguistic, social, moral, economic, scientific and cultural activities which characterize human beings in society. The '*mens*' is a second-order ability, an ability to acquire other abilities, the most important of which is mastery of language. These abilities are usually bundled together after the differentiation of reason and will. The author expressly notes that the classification [of these abilities] by a number of scholars in the tradition into cognitive and volitive abilities is supplemented by the faculty of judgement, where weighing, distinguishing, and deciding cannot do without the cognitive abilities, which are truth-related, and volitive abilities, tied to what is good.

All these abilities can only be realized through language, and cannot be separated from one another. The will cannot be thought of independently of the intellect, and the intellect cannot be employed without the will. Hence will becomes free will where action is taken for rational reasons.

The resulting identity of the person can be expressed in different roles, which he or she takes up responsibly. The person faces the challenge of creating a meaningful life within the horizons of truth and good. 'To know and to love are realizations of human identity whose epicentre lies in

---

3 Cf. GH Mead, E*spíritu, persona y sociedad*, Buenos Aires 1973.

two opposing points: when it is a question of consciousness, the epicentre is found *in the one who loves*; when it is about love, *it is found in the beloved*. Knowing means being in the other in the same way as one is within oneself; loving means being in one's self as one is in the other.'[4]

I and Thou, the Other and I, form a reciprocal relationship of a constitutive nature. At the same time, the fulfilment and realization of their unity keeps the different beings separate.

From these basic insights into human subjectivity, the author deals with today's philosophical reflections on the human '*mens*': behavioural-psychological and logical approaches (W. Watson, B.F. Skinner, G. Ryle), monistic identity theories (R. Rorty, Feieraband etc.), functionalism (Hillary Putnam, Jerry Fodor) and the various approaches to emergence.

In his concluding summary, the author formulates theses in which – in contrast to the 'total claim' that I am my body/I have a body – he presents the corresponding overall claim regarding the human being: man is spirit / man has a spirit.

- 'The spirit (or spirituality [*Espiritualidad*] in the sense of the spiritual nature) of man does not signify an independent part of man, but his wholeness: the spirit is incarnated and embodied.'
- 'The spirit designates the dimension of man that is specific to man: his intelligence, his will, his freedom, his consciousness, his *mens*, the

4 G Amengual, *Antropólogia filosófica*, cit., 190.

realization of which is always in and through the body.'
- 'Spirit designates the principle of action in man that cannot be traced back to pure biology, even though he always acts thanks to and in connection with it; these are processes that cannot be traced back to purely natural processes, because intelligence, consciousness, freedom, chosen values, creativity are incorporated.'
- 'The subjective and personal nature of the human being is defined by the spirit, by turning back on oneself, by inwardness. It is man as spirit who can claim that he has a body and that "I am my body"'.
- 'So spirit refers to the radical opening of man to reality and to being, which gives the characteristic ability for knowledge, freedom and which opens him up to truth and the good.'[5]

In terms of the concept of the person, Amengual offers an excellent overview of the history of the term and the meaning of person, starting from its Latin origins and biblical roots, then moving on to Christianity, the Middle Ages and modern times up to German idealism. He develops the current state of the discussion from Scheler on the one hand and Strawson on the other.[6]

5  G AMENGUAL, *Antropólogia filosófica*, cit., 204.
6  For this the author bases himself on the following editions in Spanish: M SCHELER, *El puesto de l'hombre en el cosmos,* Buenos Aires 1981; *Etica. Nuevo ensajo de fundamentación de un personalismo*

In the case of Scheler, the author emphasizes in particular the numerous ways in which the person proves to be an active centre of actions that are forged by the spirit and in which the person shows himself to be a subject.

With regard to Strawson, his crisis is centred on the characterization of the person through predicates of a material and personal nature which are attributed to states of consciousness and to expressing bodily characteristics.

There are many other questions and concepts that follow those of the phenomenological and analytical kind, first of all as an approach to a concept of person – which essentially is described, not defined – capable of protecting the individuality of human existence as a unity, and in particular the unity and uniqueness of individuals, despite their belonging to a unique human species. This unique individuality, which is immediately apparent through spiritual acts, forbids our understanding the person as subjectivity which only realizes itself through acts: rather is the human being a person and becomes this or that kind of person through acting in freedom.

Follow-up questions in the field of analytical philosophy refer, inter alia, to the distinction between being ourselves and selfhood (*mismidad*, *ipseidad*), and the different kinds of otherness that are found, as determination of the moment of universal relationship or its negation.

*etico*, Madrid 2001; Also PF STRAWSON, *Individuos. Ensajo de metafísica descriptiva*, Madrid 1989.

Amengual sums up his reflections and critical synthesis as follows:

> The person appears to us to be someone who is being-in-the-world, corporeal, social, gifted with language, feelings, aware and intelligent, and we also consider person for its development as a subject in identity, a subject who is free, active and passive, who is formed and always develops within a specific culture, who must build a society in which to be part of ... in all the essential features of human existence we have mentioned, the person shows a radical openness to the other which is a sign of openness to the totally Other, the Sacred, the Mystery.[7]

b) Consciousness, spirit, and person in Pope Francis' theological anthropology.

If we examine Pope Francis' magisterial texts, guided by the question of how the texts reflect the philosophical issues discussed in this section, the Encyclical *LF* on faith gives rise to the expectation that we will find them here, especially in Chapter Two entitled 'Unless you believe you will not understand' (cf. Is 7:9): well then, we will say, here it speaks of faith and truth, of the knowledge of truth and love, of faith as hearing and seeing, of dialogue between faith and religion, of faith and the search for God, of faith and theology.

---

7  G AMENGUAL, *Antropología filosófica, cit.*, 233-234.

After an historical introduction, the second chapter poses the question of 'the kind of knowledge involved in faith' (*LF*, no. 26). The answer is:

> The heart is the core of the human person, where all his or her different dimensions intersect: body and spirit, interiority and openness to the world and to others, intellect, will and affectivity. If the heart is capable of holding all these dimensions together, it is because it is where we become open to truth and love, where we let them touch us and deeply transform us. (*ivi*)

How is the heart defined? First of all as the centre where all the 'dimensions' intersect, meaning the fundamental features of human being-there which create these dimensions and where these, when realized, intersect without being transformed into something else. It is a little like lines intersecting at a point, but they have their principle of unity in their plurality. In what follows, the heart is understood as fundamentally capable of 'holding all these dimensions together,' which means it leads them to unity and to cooperate. This capability is based on the fact that the heart is the place 'where we become open to truth and love.'

These statements (opening to truth, opening to love) are ones we have already found in the philosophical reflections on anthropology, but as the fruit of a long process of mediation which first of all considered the immediacy of consciousness, the mediated reflection then made possible by this, the unfolding of selfhood and encounter with others in their world apart. Hence the questions of truth and love came into play, with different emphases, as a state of being and being in self or in the other.

It has also been said that in this entire process we are dealing with being 'touched' and being 'transformed'. The curious detachment of the statements on faith that is united to love becomes clear when we read, in what follows, what the foundation of this affinity is: 'Faith knows because it is tied to love, because love itself brings enlightenment' (*LF*, no. 26). Here faith becomes a subject who acts, as love which brings enlightenment. It is not an I or a Thou who believes one or other thing and loves it. Faith is totally objectified.[8] Instead, if we move on to other magisterial documents by Pope Francis, the strong points of philosophical reflection take on another whole presence. They are not skipped over, emerge naturally, not in philosophical reflection but in real situations which are dealt with immediately. By way of illustration, let us take a look at nos 88-92 of *EG* which speak of the relationships in and through which the faith is communicated and the gospel transmitted.

> The Christian ideal will always be a summons to overcome suspicion, habitual mistrust, fear of losing our privacy, all the defensive attitudes

---

8  Here we gain the strong impression that the text goes back once again to Pope Benedict and those who collaborated with him in establishing the Year of Faith. The features of the text we have observed here correspond oddly enough to the whole journey of the 'Year of Faith'. Regarding this cf. the critical stance on the Year of Faith taken by S WENDEL: 'Handle danach, und du wirst leben' – Ein Rückblick auf das "Jahr des Glaubens" in *Herder Korrespondenz,* 67 (2103), 565-569.

which today's world imposes on us. Many try to escape from others and take refuge in the comfort of their privacy or in a small circle of close friends, renouncing the realism of the social aspect of the Gospel. For just as some people want a purely spiritual Christ, without flesh and without the cross, they also want their interpersonal relationships provided by sophisticated equipment, by screens and systems which can be turned on and off on command. Meanwhile, the Gospel tells us constantly to run the risk of a face-to-face encounter with others, with their physical presence which challenges us, with their pain and their pleas, with their joy which infects us in our close and continuous interaction. True faith in the incarnate Son of God is inseparable from self-giving, from membership in the community, from service, from reconciliation with others. The Son of God, by becoming flesh, summoned us to the revolution of tenderness (*EG* no. 88).

In this case the other is spoken of in terms of an individual, a Thou, someone with a face, a bodily presence, someone who suffers, has aspirations, infectious joy. This person is there in all his or her affections. This other thirsts for salvation, wants to be free, seeks to live with others in a companionable way. Only at this level of dialogue, in the room provided by trust that allows one to open oneself, to pour out ones heart, can one bring faith in God to the other, faith in the Father who loves Jesus Christ. In this context the text says expressly:

> In this preaching, which is always respectful and gentle, the first step is personal dialogue, when the other person speaks and shares his or her joys, hopes and concerns for loved ones, or so many other heartfelt needs. Only afterwards is it possible to bring up God's word, perhaps by reading a Bible verse or relating a story, but always keeping in mind the fundamental message: the personal love of God who became man, who gave himself up for us, who is living and who offers us his salvation and his friendship. This message has to be shared humbly as a testimony on the part of one who is always willing to learn, in the awareness that the message is so rich and so deep that it always exceeds our grasp (*EG*, no 128).

Thus the partners in this dialogue 'will have an experience of being listened to and understood; they will know that their particular situation has been placed before God, and that God's word really speaks to their lives' (*ivi*).

This attitude, this openness and the resulting mediation of the faith must also shape the community of believers who, in the words of Pope Francis, are 'a mystical fraternity, a contemplative fraternity. It is a fraternal love capable of seeing the sacred grandeur of our neighbour, of finding God in every human being, of tolerating the nuisances of life in common by clinging to the love of God, of opening the heart to divine love and seeking the happiness of others just as their heavenly Father does' (*EG*, no. 92). In this sense, the community of believers is 'the salt of the earth and the light of the world.'

Thus, the basic features of philosophical anthropology are reflected, as it were, in two versions in Pope Francis' teaching about faith: on the one hand, the description of suffering and evil in personal and social life and on the other, the description of the respective challenges of the gospel and its examples which he takes from the life of Christian communities and individual believers. Both the list of anthropological distortions and correct application help him to present these insights in terms of modern philosophical anthropology, which Gabriel Amengual has worked out from numerous anthropological publications in the form of a structural phenomenology of the human being. His familiarity with these developments of modern anthropology helps Pope Francis – with regard to social phenomena in particular – to adequately identify the threats to Church and society. For example, in *EG* he speaks of a 'spiritual worldliness' manifesting itself today in the Church as the ultimate harmful thing to the life of faith:

> This worldliness can be fuelled in two deeply interrelated ways. One is the attraction of gnosticism, a purely subjective faith whose only interest is a certain experience or a set of ideas and bits of information which are meant to console and enlighten, but which ultimately keep one imprisoned in his or her own thoughts and feelings. The other is the self-absorbed

promethean neopelagianism of those who ultimately trust only in their own powers and feel superior to others because they observe certain rules or remain intransigently faithful to a particular Catholic style from the past. A supposed soundness of doctrine or discipline leads instead to a narcissistic and authoritarian elitism, whereby instead of evangelizing, one analyzes and classifies others, and instead of opening the door to grace, one exhausts his or her energies in inspecting and verifying. In neither case is one really concerned about Jesus Christ or others. These are manifestations of an anthropocentric immanentism. It is impossible to think that a genuine evangelizing thrust could emerge from these adulterated forms of Christianity (*EG*, no. 94).[9]

---

9   In comments that follow, the Pope mentions a whole range of ways of behaving in the Church which stem from this fundamental worldliness. Cf. *EG* nos 95-101.

Chapter 5
# A LOOK AT THE CURRENT SITUATION GIVEN THE BASICS OF HUMAN EXISTENCE

*1. Some prior notes on method*

In the preceding chapters we have kept strictly to the *modus operandi* described at the beginning. This approach has helped us to discover the basics features of modern anthropology as developed in philosophy, in the Pope's proclamation of the faith. In this final chapter too, the comparison between a philosophical and theological viewpoint will be maintained, although with substantial modifications.

As we did earlier, we will certainly call on philosophical notions presented by Amengual in his second part. He describes his theme in this chapter with the keyword 'determination'; and, by contrast with the explanation of structures or basic features of modern philosophocal anthropology, he now explains that he will speak about 'the capacities and processes which now place the human being in the foreground as existence, as a project, as a process of development.'[1] By dealing especially with the freedom achieved, and indeed by seeing it as the decisive dynamic in this process, a contemporary reference of a special kind

1 G AMENGUAL, *Antropología filosófica, cit., 239.*

comes into these presentations. Philosophical reflections and phenomenological analyses cannot capture the empirical event. But there are some structures of human liberty typical of our age which can give a foundation to empirical practice and manifest themselves in it.

If we now look at the content which Amengual deals with in the second part of his presentation – after the two introductory chapters on human identity communicated freely, and freedom as transcendental anthropological determination[2] – he offers reflections on human action, forms of labour, including modern forms of work, technology and leisure. Amengual then speaks of historicity, that takes on an important role in culture, and concludes his remarks with a very brief section on building a society in solidarity.

If we compare these topics, which are typical of contemporary times, with the statements of Pope Francis in *Evangelii Gaudium*, *Laudato Di'* and *Amoris Laetitia*, then there are serious differences. In the second chapter of *EG*, Pope Francis speaks of the current crisis of social life and says "No to an economy of exclusion; no to the new idolatry of money; no to a financial system which rules rather than serves; no to the inequality which spawns violence.' This is followed by a section on the challenges of urban cultures. In the third chapter of *LS* dedicated to the human roots of the ecological crisis he addresses in particular: 1. Technology: creativity and power; 2. The globalization of the technocratic paradigm; 3. The crisis and effects of

---

2   Here the author arrives at the narrative identity of Ricoeur and thinkers like Zubiri.

modern anthropocentrism. In *AL*, in the second chapter he deals with the 'current reality of the family' exploring the anthropological and cultural changes and social tendencies or structures that essentially endanger and threaten the present situation of the family.

These are typical of contemporary issues that shape anthropology.

It would seem unreasonable to use philosophical anthropology in this area as a point of reference for the presentation of relevant facts in Francis' theological anthropology. The reason for this cannot simply be attributed to the author of *Antropología filosófica*. A glance at terms like 'money' or 'economy' in the much renowned and extensive *Historisches Wörterbuch der Philosophie* offers us, in the case of the first of these, a brief article and very few names of philosophers who have taken a particular position on all this. In the case of the other term we find, for example, only a relatively short article on ethics in economy, in which key authors of the Catholic social doctrine and the subsequent evangelical social teaching occupy a prominent place.

We will take account of these changed relationships between philosophical and theological anthropology in this chapter by providing, on the one hand, a very brief summary of the relevant philosophical doctrines proposed, and, on the other, accompany the presentation of corresponding issues in Pope Francis' doctrinal texts with the question of what lies behind these statements which are, of course, essential for theological anthropology.

## 2. *The current social scene from the point of view of theological anthropology*

Before beginning our presentation, we need to free ourselves from a misunderstanding: it is not a question of asking the philosopher for a presentation of the social scene from a sociological point of view, but rather of learning what he has to say as a philosopher concerning the process that human beings realize by existing here and now in our time.

A first answer comes from the first two chapters: first of all identity, be it especially personal identity, or group identity, always understood as being in a process of construction.

'Identity is not a collection of special traits possessed by the individual. It is the ego understood reflectively by the person, autobiographically.'[3] This encompasses the consciousness of identity in time and space. Just as in this unity, however, the events that take place are integrated and to be integrated into the whole biographical continuity, and so identity is identification with a culture, a group, etc. But this identity is always in a process of formation. The author takes an historical approach, through suggestions made by philosophers, especially in recent times by Erik H. Erikson. He makes a comparison with a series of analytical philosophers who are inspired by Strawson and finally comes to narrative identity as conceived by Paul Ricoeur.[4] He sums it up as follows: '1. The ego is not something immediate,

---

3 G AMENGUAL, *Antropología filosófica*, cit., 243.
4 Cf. P Ricoeur, *Oneself as another*, University of Chicago Press, 1992.

but the result of mediation and reflection. 2. The dialectic between selfhood and otherness belongs to personal identity. Otherness is constitutive of selfhood itself.'[5] Both moments also arise in the context of groups of people who form their identities - a specific We - in the same way.

The second key statement in relation to the human being, humanity in its being-there, which the philosopher gives – the author here takes up Hegel's statement in a slightly modified form – is: 'The essence of man is freedom.'[6] The author describes the philosophical understandings of antiquity and the Middle Ages up to Heidegger and then speaks of freedom as an 'anthropological transcendental'.[7] In doing so, he distinguishes the freedom of being or the *constitutive* freedom of man from the freedom of acting.[8] In this sense he is describing freedom as the ability to realize the totality and definiteness of human existence.[9] Finally, he speaks of the transcendental of freedom through contact with the mystery: 'In this openness, characteristic of freedom ... man experiences his original being touched by the mystery that embraces the whole of man's existence which we call God, and which is always already found in this openness of freedom and the experience of freedom.

---

5   G AMENGUAL, *Antropología filosófica*, cit., 255.
6   In fact Hegel is talking about the essence of the spirit, cf., *Ibidem*, 257.
7   *Ibidem*, 269.
8   Here the author is picking up an expression of Johann Baptist Metz: *Freiheit als philosophisch-theologisches Grenzproblem, in Gott in Welt, FS für Karl Rahner, Freiburg 1964*, 287–314.
9   G AMENGUAL, *Antropología filosófica*, cit., 273

Moreover, when man hears the call to accountability within freedom, then he experiences this as a demand, as a call to this mystery.'[10]

Against this background of man's being-in-the-world, of his personal identity and freedom with regard to his personal and social existence, the author offers the reader an overview of how work and technology are looked at today. He goes from the philosophy of action of Greek philosophy in antiquity (*poiesis* and *praxis*), to the personal and social nature of action, then to early descriptions of work as *labor improbus* and 'free activity' – not without the mediation of Christianity. Along with Hegel and his master-servant dialectic, he describes modern work as what characterizes man, which Marx then interprets as the transformation of social structures. Only later does Amengual add reflections on technology which as a tool leads first of all to the production of instruments, and finally he speaks of the fusion of science and technology, interpreting them, along with Habermas: '[Rationality] has less to do with the recognition and appropriation of knowledge than with the way in which the subjects who are capable of speech and action apply the knowledge.'[11] This then means that today's culture consists of life in the 'technopolis', the culture in which people live today. It is shaped in all respects by the technologies that determine people's way of life and thinking. It develops,

10  *Ibidem*, 275.
11  Quoted from *Ibidem*, 303, taken from J HABERMAS, *Theorie des kommunikativen Handelns*, Frankfurt am Main 1981, 2 vols.

on the other hand, in different forms, because culture is characterized by different habitats and historical traditions.

### 3. *The current social situation evaluated in* Evangelii Gaudium, Laudato Si' *and* Amoris Laetita

Reference has already been made in this context to the passages from Pope Francis' doctrinal texts which are the object of our investigation. They will be presented below with particular emphasis on *Evangelii Gaudium*.

First of all we quoted the second chapter of the Apostolic Exhortation *EG*. The introduction to this chapter deals with the theological approaches underlying his assessment of the current social situation. In order to tackle basic questions related to the work of evangelization, it is necessary to 'mention briefly the context in which we all have to live and work' (*EG*, no. 50). This is how he defines the task. Does this mean that the Pope is requesting further sociological studies in order to bring a new solution to resolve the thoroughly controversial assessment? This is not his purpose and intention. Francis refers to the 'diagnostic overload' that is not always accompanied by really applicable solutions. This only leads to an 'allegedly neutral and clinical method.' Rather, Pope Francis wants to make a spiritual decision on the basis of the gospel and to be guided by the 'signs of the times'. He expressly refuses to offer 'a detailed and complete analysis of contemporary reality.' At the same time, he clearly sees signs in the situation or circumstances 'since certain present realities, unless effectively dealt with, are capable of setting off processes of dehumanization which would then be hard to reverse.' Beginning with these signs, 'we need to distinguish clearly what might be a fruit of the kingdom from what runs counter to God's plan' (*EG*, nos. 50-51).

Discernment of spirits is a term which belongs to the monastic spiritual tradition and was picked up once more by Ignatius of Loyola in his *Spiritual Exercises*, where the discussion is about deciding in practical terms for a life dedicated to the glory of God according to ones personal calling, and in particular, by considering concrete possibilities.

The concept of discernment of spirits was introduced by John XXIII during the work of the Second Vatican Council (*Gaudium et Spes*, no. 4, *GS*). In *GS*, it is described thus: 'the Church has always had the duty of scrutinizing the signs of the times and of interpreting them in the light of the gospel. Thus, in language intelligible to each generation, she can respond to the perennial questions which men ask about this present life and the life to come, and about the relationship of the one to the other. We must therefore recognize and understand the world in which we live, its explanations, its longings, and its often dramatic characteristics' (*GS*, no. 4).

This information is for the most part foreign to us moderns, since it comes from an ecclesiastical tradition with which we are unfamiliar and therefore suspicious of. What is hidden in these words? In a few concise lines, based on his position on the social situation – as it was characterized in the context of philosophical anthropology by speaking of the 'Technopolis' – Francis outlines what these words and practical instructions mean for him.

First of all (*EG*, no. 52), he describes the turning-point in history which people today are experiencing: 'We can only praise the steps being taken to improve people's welfare in areas such as health care, education and communications.' Other things could be added to these examples, such as the improved situation of well-being for so many people. But it is especially in relation to modern technologies and the emergence of the 'technopolis,' as well as the decisive power of technology to shape culture in more profound ways, that a process of 'exclusion' comes into play (*EG*, no. 53). Because the formation of the 'technopolis' is a still developing historical process, the problem arises of how people can be integrated into this process and are de facto integrated or excluded on the basis of their origins, education, etc. For once excluded, there are virtually no real opportunities for people to integrate themselves into the 'technopolis'.

And at this point, Pope Francis has something new to say: 'Exclusion ultimately has to do with what it means to be a part of the society in which we live; those excluded are no longer society's underside or its fringes or its disenfranchised – they are no longer even a part of it. The excluded are not the "exploited" but the outcast, the "leftovers"' (*EG*, no. 53). This is the real situation for many men and women today. But they live under the gaze of the inhabitants of the 'technopolis', who often no longer see them: they have become indifferent to them,[12] because all their vital energy

---

12 In *EG*, no. 54, Francis speaks of the 'globalization of indifference': 'Almost without being aware of it, we end up being incapable of feeling compassion at the outcry of the poor, weeping

is taken up in the living conditions and structures of the 'technopolis'.

Personal questions arise from this, as to what and how the individual can act, or how he or she acts *de facto*, here and now, to counter this ever more consistent risk of dehumanization. No longer is it a question of: 'What should be done?', but 'What should I do?', 'What should we do?' A decision is made through discernment of spirits. The same structure and argumentation presented in relation to the economy and technocracy is applied in relation to the socially-established monetary system. In the financial system itself, there is a strong move to the 'idolatry of money' inasmuch as this system dominates over other contexts in the system through its vast concentration of power. 'Money rules the world.' It is a struggle for regulatory procedures and state laws to keep the whole banking system useful, while keeping the common good in mind and trying not to facilitate the creation of huge assets.

Francis' third example, finally, is the 'No' to be said to social inequality that produces violence. This reflects the rich experiences he has had in Latin America and the social issues that are central to that.

Such arguments in the context of a theological anthropology assume familiarity with the great developments of human history, which can be grasped through philosophy

---

for other people's pain, and feeling a need to help them, as though all this were someone else's responsibility and not our own... In the meantime all those lives stunted for lack of opportunity seem a mere spectacle; they fail to move us.'

and which sociology and other sciences can provide a foundation for.

Secondly, such reasoning assumes that the inner limit of a liberal, human development process is seen and evaluated. But the limit shows itself precisely to those who have been harmed, hindered, rejected. The 'option for the poor' comes into its own here. Thirdly, this also assumes that moral assessment, the assessment of good and evil, is included in this formation of judgement – before 'God's face', that is, before a supreme good which has not been determined ideologically, but which arises from human freedom to which unconditional assent is given.

Jesus' view of this human situation, the view the disciples had in faith proves, from a formal perspective, to be a view capable of seeing both the transcendental and empirical facts together, and at the same time this view is characterized by its 'theoretical' and 'practical' unity, meaning it is an ethical point of view in a way that it does not confuse these different perspectives, thus leading to misleading conclusions.

With regard to the above-mentioned remarks on the human root of the ecological crisis in the Encyclical *LS*, the same structure is used to argue the point – sometimes with slightly different emphases. Pope Francis speaks of the development of technoscience, which has produced countless good effects, but at the same time also represents a hitherto unknown accumulation of power that lies in the hands of the few and determines the global future. However, the resulting ecological crisis can not simply be resolved by 'a technical remedy to each environmental problem which comes up' (*LS*, no. 111). The remedy can only be applied in such a way that it is at the service of the human being by transforming lifestyles, constantly renewing technology, and other appropriate forms. 'An authentic humanity, calling for a new synthesis, seems to dwell in the midst of our technological culture, almost unnoticed, like a mist seeping gently beneath a closed door' (*LS*, no. 112). This can only emerge from a new, all-encompassing spirituality, based on discernment of spirits and its corresponding actions in everyday life and in major public issues. This is where the remarks in *AL* concerning the crisis of marriage and questions about the success of Christian marriage seem to be most appropriate.

# CONCLUDING NOTE

The title of this study is *Human beings according to Christ today. Pope Francis' Anthropology*. The answer to this question has been developed through a critical and systematic process of investigation and it is as follows: Pope Francis' texts of doctrinal proclamation demonstrate a well-rounded, new and modern form of theological anthropology which at the same time reveals its own methodology.

From this – but this cannot be developed here – come new understandings and interpretations of the great masterpieces of philosophical reflection by Plato and Aristotle as well as theological reflection by Thomas Aquinas, on human being-there [*Da-Sein*]. These things were neither seen by Enlightenment philosophy nor by Baroque Scholasticism or Neo-Scholasticism. This new theological anthropology displays considerable differences to the traditional form. As far as I can see, its acceptance and development in today's dogmatics and proclamation is only at the beginning. Pope Francis' pioneering magisterial texts point out the direction to be followed.

www.ingramcontent.com/pod-product-compliance
Lightning Source LLC
Chambersburg PA
CBHW052028290426
44112CB00014B/2428